MW00415143

Praise for
Go! How to Find and Pursue Your Passionate Purpose

"If you want to win in business and in life, you've got to be intentional. Nobody succeeds by accident or stumbles into a fulfilling life. You've got to put some work into it! In *Go!*, Greg shows you the steps you need to make the most out of your life. It's a great game plan filled with things that I've been doing for years. Don't miss it!"

--Dave Ramsey
New York Times best-selling author and nationally syndicated radio show host

"We are often reminded that many people die with their music still in them. Don't let that be said of you. In this delightful book, Greg shows you how to tap into the "music" that only you are prepared to share with the world. Be the maestro God intended you to be."

--Dan Miller
New York Times bestselling author of 48 Days to the Work You Love

"Are you tired of feeling 'trapped' when you know that life has so much more to offer? Or perhaps you are on the right track, but you want to accelerate your journey to success and significance? Then you need to pick up and devour *Go! How to Find and Pursue Your Passionate Purpose*. by Greg Knapp today! And never forget: Change starts with you, but it doesn't start until you do."

--Tom Ziglar
CEO of Ziglar, Inc.

"Skip right to chapter 6 on mindset. It's my favorite!"

--Andy Traub
Author of The Early To Rise Experience

"Everyone is created with a God-given purpose. If you're not living it, you know something is missing. Pursuing it is the path to fulfillment, success, helping others, and significance. Greg helps you find that purpose that's always been inside you and then gives you the tools to Go!"

--Harold Finch

Project Director, NASA, Apollo Heating Program, lunar spacecraft missions, Founder of Padgett-Thompson, Founder of CottageCare

"If you really want to fulfill your own Passionate Purpose, read this book. Greg has lived and breathed the principles it contains and used them for his own success. You can, too. Well-written. Motivating. The best motivational book on the market."

--Dave Lapham
Award-winning author

"This book is a winner! Greg not only helps people discover their dreams, he also walks them through how to accomplish them. The step-by-step format is great. I love that it's not just a collection of motivational sayings. There's a true method involved."

--Tim Howey
Founder and Sr. Pastor of Grace Church, Overland Park, KS

"In the Marine Corps, the drill instructors demanded, 'Lead, Follow, or Get Out of the Way!' Greg gives us a map and compass to lead—not others—but ourselves—to the top of our hill, to achieve our own passionate purpose."

--John Brunner
Former CEO of Vi-Jon, Marine and philanthropist

"Have you ever felt frustrated or stuck, like you are going through the motions, but not sure toward what? Greg helps you find or rediscover your passion and actually take steps to act on it. Read Go! today so you can feel excited and inspired to get moving purposefully!"

--Jody Cross
Speaker & Best Selling Author, Leaders Speak

Go!

How to Find and Pursue Your Passionate Purpose

Gregory B. Knapp, M.A.

Copyright 2015 Gregory B. Knapp

All rights reserved

Printed in the United States of America

No part of this publication may be reproduced, stored in or introduced into a retrieval system, or transmitted, in any form, or by any means (electronic, mechanical, photocopying, recording, or otherwise), without the prior permission of the author.

Dreaming Big, Inc.

ISBN-13: 978-1505842807
ISBN-10: 1505842808

To my wife, Anne, for listening to all my crazy ideas and actually supporting most of them. You are the kindest person I have ever met, and I love you. To my daughters, Faith and Summer, for your encouragement and for all the joy you bring to my life.

Contents

Why Are You Reading This?

The Right Answer Will Change Your Life

The two most important days in your life are the day you are born and the day you find out why.

–Mark Twain, American author and humorist

Stop. For a second stop, think, and really answer this question:

Why are you reading this right now?

Your life will, or won't, change based on your answer. You spent your valuable money to buy this book and you are now investing your even more valuable, limited time to read it. You expect to get something out of it.

What do you want? Why?

Maybe we are a lot alike. You have this feeling deep inside you, that you were made for something better. You're in the midst of an existential crisis where you realize this is it. *This* is your life—right now. You don't get a dress rehearsal or a do-over. You get one shot at it and it's not going the way you want it to go. You want more out of life. You can't stand the idea of being average, mediocre, or just getting by.

You're tired of just settling, tired of putting aside your dreams, tired of accepting the conventional wisdom that life is hard and only the lucky few really enjoy it.

You want to break free from the opiates of our society that are keeping you from achieving the success that somehow you know you were born for. You're tired of distracting yourself with television, surfing the web, checking your Facebook, Twitter, Instagram and Google Plus accounts to see if your virtual life is better than your real one.

You want to break away from the 95 percent who half-heartedly go to work every day to earn a living. You want to do what you are passionate about and make a life.

You understand that every day that goes by is gone forever and you have a limited amount of time on this planet. Knowing this, you don't want to just get *through* the day. You want to wake up looking forward to what you're going to get *out* of the day. You want to feel like a kid on Christmas morning *every day* because you can't wait to start the next part of your life.

The idea of looking at each day just as something to survive has always seemed defeatist to you. You want to create a life worth living, one precious moment at a time.

You want to enjoy every part of your life. You believe God created you for a reason. You want your life to have meaning. You want to make a difference. You want to have an impact on the world and on the people you love. You want to leave a legacy. You want to give to others. You want to live with a Passionate Purpose™.

You want to dream big and enjoy the whole journey while you pursue those dreams and fulfill your destiny.

You want to be excited about your career, your spouse, your relationships, your family, your spiritual development, and your physical body.

But you want even more than that. You want *freedom*—freedom to control your own time, schedule, work, vacation, and life. You want to travel the world with the people you love. You want to generate abundant amounts of income so you can do everything you've ever dreamed of. You want to take care of your family and give to help others. You want to reach your full potential and suck the juice out of every part of your life so that when you die everyone at your funeral says, "Wow, that dude *lived*."

Oh, is that all? I hope you want all that *and more*. Isn't *that* why you are reading this? What if I told you, you *can* have all that … depending on how you answer my question?

Why are you reading this?

You *Must* Change

If you are reading this hoping to get motivated and maybe get a couple of neat ideas, that will be fun and interesting for you. But it won't change your life. It won't get you what you really want.

The only way to get the results you want and change your life forever, to live with Passionate Purpose and to enjoy the extraordinary life of your dreams, is to convince yourself that you *have* to do it.

Not that it would be nice, or fun, or kinda neat to have all that. No. You *must* have it. To not have it you would experience tremendous pain. To have it you would experience tremendous pleasure.

Convince me. Convince *yourself.*

Why? Because the first step to changing is making sure you really want to change. That core belief that you can't keep living this way and that you *must* change is what will sustain you through all the work you will need to do in order to create your new life.

The reality is that no one changes you. You change yourself. Others can assist you, but ultimately you are the one who does the hard work to create lasting change.

Have you ever thought about changing something in your life and you never quite seemed to do it? Maybe it was a new diet or exercise program. Or, perhaps, it was getting that extra degree, learning to ballroom dance, or starting your own business.

Could it be the reason you didn't accomplish your goal was that you never got to the point where you believed you *must* do it? After all, your life isn't that bad. You're making decent money, you're not morbidly obese, and most people don't go ballroom dancing anymore.

I've experienced this and I bet you have too.

My background is in psychology. I have a master's degree in counseling psychology and I became a certified behavior analyst. I used to do mental health counseling and behavior therapy for children and their families. In my experience I found that an old psychology joke was absolutely true.

> Q: How many psychologists does it take to change a light bulb?
>
> A: Only one … but the light bulb has to *want* to change.

It's true, but it's even worse than that. I'm changing the punch line:

> Q: How many psychologists does it take to change a light bulb?
>
> A: Only one … but the light bulb has to believe it *must* change.

I specialized in helping children with behavior problems. This always involved changing the parents as much as the child. I would spend most of my family counseling sessions in the home with the parents and the children. After spending time observing the family dynamics, I would help the parents develop a behavior modification plan for the child. If you ever saw the television show *Supernanny,* you have a pretty good idea of what I did. The only difference was most of my families were ordered into treatment by the court, and they lived in homes you thought were abandoned.

After working with countless families it got to the point that I could tell at the first session how successful therapy was going to be.

If the parents were in a situation where they had convinced themselves that things MUST change with their child, I knew we were going to succeed. If the parents were there just going through the motions, I knew it was not going to end well.

An extreme example is when I did an in-home session with a single mother. She was court ordered to do therapy and behavior intervention with me because of her son. He was having horrible behavior problems at home and at school, and was at risk for being removed from the home by the state. As I sat down to interview her, she turned on the television to watch Oprah. I explained to her that the television would distract us. I asked her how important her son was to her. She said she cared about him deeply, but she watched Oprah every day and couldn't turn her off. I even scheduled our appointments around Oprah and she still kept the television on. Things went downhill from there.

Another family, in almost the same situation, had a mother and child who both convinced me on day one that they had to change. They were highly emotional about how bad their relationship was, and how poorly he was doing at school. They were begging for help because they didn't want to live that way for even one more day. You can guess their outcome, can't you? It was inspiring to help them.

When I had clients who wanted to change, my job was easy. When they were at the point where they had decided they needed to change my job was cake. They were so primed to do what was necessary to make their life better that all I had to do was get them moving in the right direction.

Clients who didn't want to change were virtually unreachable and got nothing out of our therapy sessions and behavior modification plans. They didn't have the drive to do the work to change.

If this isn't the first personal development book you've read and you haven't been able to make the changes you desire in your life, I think part of the problem is you haven't convinced yourself you *must* change.

> *Definiteness of purpose is the starting point of all achievement.*
>
> –W. Clement Stone, businessman, philanthropist and self-help author

But, Greg, I do want to change. That's why I'm reading your book.

Yes, you are already ahead of 90 percent of Americans on caring enough to start this process. But the difference between wanting to change and needing to change is the difference between talking about it and doing it.

Tough Love

Are you ready for some tough love? If you have tried to change before and it hasn't worked, there is really only one reason. It's not because you don't have talent—talent is overrated. Nothing in the world is more common than unsuccessful people with talent. It's not because you aren't smart enough, don't know the right people, or don't have enough money to get started. (I will prove all that to you as well.) It's not because you don't have enough time. We all have the same 24 hours in each day. If other people are doing it, with schedules busier than yours, then why can't you?

The real reason you haven't followed through on what you say you want is this: You get more out of *not* changing than you *think* you would get out of changing.

Tony Robbins puts it this way: You believe you get more pleasure and avoid more pain by staying the way you are than by doing the work necessary to change.

I know this sounds crazy but think about it. Why don't we all eat healthy and never overeat? Isn't it because we like the pleasure we get from the taste of the foods we know aren't good for us? Isn't it because of the pleasurable feeling we create in ourselves when we eat too much? Sure it makes us gain weight and maybe even feel sluggish, but doesn't the short-term pleasure overwhelm the long-term pain? I know it does for me more times than I'd like to admit. Our actions speak louder than all the diets we've ever planned to live by.

Why do you think alcoholics and drug addicts continue to use even though it's destroying their lives? Obviously addiction is a factor, but it's also because they believe the short-term pleasure they get is greater than the long-term pain. They use substances to temporarily change the way they feel, to avoid pain in their lives, to distract themselves from their problems, and to self-medicate. Even when they are losing their jobs, their spouses, their children, their friends, their homes, and their health they keep using for the short-term pleasure and the short-term escape from their pain.

Yet, many do kick their habit. How? They do it when they hit rock bottom. When they convince themselves the pain of their addiction is worse than the short-term pleasure of using and they decide they *must* change. That's when they start the difficult recovery process.

If Someone Else Can Do It, You Can Do It

OK, Greg, I buy that for eating, exercise, drinking, and drugs but that's not why I haven't changed. I haven't been able to start a business because I don't have the startup money.

Let me ask you a question. How do we have people making average salaries starting new businesses every day in this country? How do legal immigrants come here with nothing and open a business the first year they're here? I'm talking about people who do it without a loan or investors. How do they do it?

They convinced themselves they had to. They decided that to *not* put out the effort and money necessary to pursue their goal would be *more painful* than doing it. They stayed focused on the long-term pleasure they would get and how they would avoid the long-term pain of never pursuing their dreams. They found a way.

Some saved money for years that they could have used on other things. Others found a way to start it in their home and slowly build it. Others found a way to do it all online for almost nothing. The bottom line is they found a way. You can, too.

Imagine your child has a fatal illness. The doctors say she only has six months to live. But if you get her the right medicine, she will be completely cured. One problem: The medicine costs $10,000 and you're broke. No one can loan you the money. Do you think you could earn an extra ten grand in six months to save your child?

Of course you could, and you would, because you would *have* to. With that kind of effort and commitment nothing could stop you.

That's the kind of commitment you will need because deciding you must change is just part of it. You also must decide you are willing to do the work required to make the change. No one can do the work for you. No one *makes* you change. I am giving you ideas and techniques to change your life, but I can't change you. All true change will come from you.

The *Pursuit* of Happiness

> *We hold these truths to be self-evident, that all men are created equal, that they are endowed by their Creator with certain unalienable Rights, that among these are Life, Liberty and the* ***pursuit*** *of Happiness. (Emphasis added)*
>
> –The Declaration of Independence

That's an amazing idea. No other nation on the planet asserts such a natural right for its people. A right neither man nor government gave you, so neither man nor government can take it away from you. All you have to do is *pursue* it.

What are we doing with this right? Are we working with our mind, body, heart, and soul to pursue happiness? Most of us aren't. We get caught up in living our lives. We get caught up in the small things. We get caught up in the daily grind of getting up early, making breakfast, getting the kids ready for school, going to work, taking the kids to piano lessons, making dinner, doing the dishes, fixing the leaky faucet, going grocery shopping, etc. And when the morning light comes streaming in, we get up and do it again. (Thank you, Jackson Browne.)

Why Are You Reading This?

Obviously, we have to take care of our families and ourselves but when we get caught up so much in the small things, years can go by without us ever really taking the time to figure out what makes us happy and what brings us joy.

> *The American dream, to me, means having the opportunity to achieve ... because I don't think you should be guaranteed anything other than opportunity.*
>
> –Lenny Wilkens, retired basketball player, coach in the National Basketball Association, and founder of the Lenny Wilkens Foundation for Children

Have you kept a dream inside you without acting upon it? I have, and not just one dream. Yes, you can, and probably do, have multiple Passionate Purposes in your life. They may even change throughout your life. Mine have.

I have dreams of giving keynote speeches, writing books, growing my radio show, and leading seminars that help people live extraordinary lives.

I have dreams of following Christ more closely, playing guitar and singing professionally, living in my dream home on the beach, learning several languages, traveling the world, giving generously to help others, being a great husband and father, and more.

I am now actively working to pursue all these passions, but for years I wasn't pursuing any of them. I was waiting …

> and waiting …
>
> and waiting …

How much longer will you wait? Are you waiting for "someday"? There is a great scene about this in the movie *Knight and Day* with Tom Cruise as Roy Miller and Cameron Diaz as June Havens. Their characters are just getting to know each other and they are talking about their dreams. June is talking about restoring an old car in her dad's memory.

> June: "I used to think that someday when the last part went in, I would just climb into that GTO and start it up and just drive and drive and keep driving 'til I reached the tip of South America."
>
> Roy: "Ah, someday, it's a dangerous word."
>
> June: "Dangerous?"
>
> Roy: "It's really just a code for never."
>
> "I think a lot about things I haven't done. Dive in the Great Barrier Reef, ride the Orient Express, live on the Amalfi Coast with nothing but a motorcycle and a backpack, kiss a stranger on the balcony of the Hotel Du Cap …"
>
> June: "Where is that?"
>
> Roy: "The south of France. What about you? What's your list?"

What About You?

> *Don't die with your music still inside you. Listen to your intuitive inner voice and find what passion stirs your soul. Listen to that inner voice, and don't get to the end of your life and say, "What if my whole life has been wrong?"*
>
> –Dr. Wayne W. Dyer, self-help author and motivational speaker

What about you? What's your list? Great questions. Have you figured them out? Is "someday" just code for never for you? Do you want to change that? Have you taken action to begin living your dreams? Am I going to stop asking you questions for a second? Not yet.

How tragic would it be for you to never have your someday? How awful would it be for you and, really for all of us, if you die with your music still inside you?

Now is the time. Determine what you want. Set your course. Take action.

Go.

Remember this as you begin. It's not about "achieving success" or doing whatever is necessary to get as much money as you can. You may have already been down that road and found it wanting. It's about pursuing your Passionate Purpose and *enjoying every step along the way.* Pursuing your goals *is* success. It is part of the pursuit of happiness. When you do that, you will be successful and probably end up making more money as well. Sound good?

Go.

Your Life—Your goals

> *Build your own dreams, or someone else will hire you to build theirs.*
>
> –Farrah Gray, businessman, investor, author, and motivational speaker

What is *your* happiness? This process you are about to begin must be about what *you* want, not what your parents told you to be, or what society approves of, or what your spouse wants you to do. Other people's goals for you will not work long term. Their goals will not get you excited to get up early and stay up late. Their goals will not give you the little rewards you will reap all along the way that will keep you going. Their goals will not have you living a life of Passionate Purpose.

You don't want to spend years or even decades of your life pursuing what someone else wants for your life do you? Don't be the man who finally climbed the ladder of success only to find out he put it up against the wrong wall.

Is This You? Does It Have to Be?

Most people die at 25 but aren't buried until they're 75.

–Benjamin Franklin, Founding Father

A friend of mine is a financially successful lawyer. He works hard for the firm putting in 50–60 hours a week. He has a wonderful family, a nice home, and takes well-earned cruises and vacations. But one time we got into a rather deep conversation and he confessed to me that he was not happy with his work. In fact, he said he didn't really have the passion for being a lawyer anymore and wasn't sure he ever had it.

He and his wife had been volunteering with the youth group at their church. He found great joy and fulfillment in working with the teens and helping them develop their relationship with Christ. He told me that if he could, he would become a youth minister. He also thought it would help his quality of life. He could spend more time with his family. He could take better care of his health. He might even be able to get some sleep.

I asked him what was stopping him from doing exactly that. He replied that he was trapped. He had put so much time, effort, and money into getting his law degree, how could he walk away from that now? Besides, he was trapped by the bills he had to pay. All his children were in private school. He had a mortgage. His family had a certain lifestyle they had grown accustomed to. He couldn't maintain that lifestyle for his family as a youth minister.

Do you ever have thoughts like those? Do you feel trapped? Do you feel like there's no way to pursue your dreams without making sacrifices too big for you and for those you love?

I understand the need to be realistic. I don't want you to abandon all your responsibilities to chase a dream you haven't prepared for. But what if?

What if there was a way to slowly transition to your dream life? What if you could pursue your Passionate Purpose without letting your family down? What if you give your family a chance to make a few sacrifices with you so you can go after your extraordinary life? What if it ended up making everyone's life better?

What if my friend had talked to his family about how miserable he was with his job and workload? Is it possible that they would *want* him to start making changes? They love him, after all. Might they have decided private school tuition wasn't worth what the cost was for their dad? What if they said they could take fewer cruises and exotic vacations? What if they found ways to cut back on some of the luxuries they don't really need because they love him? What if my friend could go part time at the law firm and begin working part time as a youth minister? Could there be a way they could pay the bills and allow my friend to sing the song he's been keeping locked inside?

We don't know, because he never asked. He still works at the same firm, putting in the same crazy schedule. He still looks beaten down most of the time when I see him. He still has *30 more years* of feeling trapped before he finally retires.

Is that you? Does it have to be?

Now Is the Time

The most difficult thing is the decision to act, the rest is merely tenacity.

–Amelia Earhart, American aviation pioneer and author

It's time to convince yourself these aren't just wants, they are needs. If you are tired of just getting by and letting days, months, and years slip by without achieving what you know you were put on this earth by your Creator to do, then now is the time.

If you answer my question correctly, then we will discover your Passionate Purpose, set your goals, and develop short- and long-term plans to get there. We will develop ways to stay motivated and live the life you've always dreamed of, and you were designed for.

You will probably have one overriding Passionate Purpose with several underlying Passionate Purposes. We want to find the purposes for every part of your life. However, to keep it simple, I will refer to your Passionate Purposes in the singular form throughout the book.

Ready?

Go!

What Do You Truly Want?

The First Step to Finding Your Passionate Purpose

You've got to be very careful if you don't know where you are going because you might not get there.

–Yogi Berra, former Major League Baseball catcher, manager, and coach.

Most people have dreams, wishes, hopes, fantasies, sometimes even delusions, but no concrete idea of what they truly want.

They don't ever take the time to think about it. They just do what they think they're supposed to do. Go to school. Graduate. Go to college. Graduate. Get a job. Work it. Get married. Have kids. Keep working your job. Buy stuff and fill what little leisure time you have with everything you can to make you "happy."

Most people drift through life with no fixed destination in mind, making do with whatever comes their way. If you take a trip with no particular place to go, that's where you end up—no particular place. Is that where you want to be?

Some people move past that and get an idea of what they really want. A few even create a real goal. But even fewer follow through with a plan and take the consistent action necessary to reach that goal.

You are here to be one of the few, the proud, the Goal Achievers. (Goal Warriors? Goaldiers? OK, I'll keep working on it.)

In the next several chapters you will learn how to do three things to get you on your path:

1. *Find your Passionate Purpose*

2. *Set your goals*

3. *Go!*

Most American Workers Don't Even Like Their Jobs

Newsflash: You do not equal your job. Sure, you already knew that. Everybody says that. But do we really mean it? We've been taught since we were little that your identity is your job. When you were asked in school, "What do you want to be when you grow up?" everybody knew it really meant, "What job do you want?"

We have created a connection between what we do to earn an income and who we are. Is that currently a healthy connection for you? Unfortunately, it isn't for most Americans.

A 2013 Gallup Poll showed only 30 percent of Americans were excited about their jobs. Are you one of the 70 percent who aren't? Are you one of the 18 percent the poll showed to be so disgruntled at your job that you are "actively disengaged"? That sounds like a fun way to spend 40-60 hours a week, doesn't it?

How can so many of us become resigned to the fact that we hate what we spend a majority of our waking time doing? Is it any wonder we have problems with depression, alcohol, drugs, and whatever other means we can use to escape the drudgery of our daily work lives?

Even though you do not equal your job, wouldn't it be nice to figure out what gets you excited and then find a way to turn that into your career?

I Don't Want to Work If It Means Hating My Job

> *I've been lazy most all of my life, writing songs and sleeping late. Any manual labor I've done purely by mistake.*
>
> –Jimmy Buffet, singer, songwriter, and businessman, from the song "It's My Job"

As far back as I can remember I did not want to work. I wanted to play and spend my time doing the things I loved to do. At the age of five, I announced to my mother that I wanted to become a kindergarten teacher because they only taught half days (Hey, I only went for half the day, so I figured the teacher went home when I did. Remember, I was five.) After watching the movie *The Sting* at the age of seven, I told my dad I wanted to be a con artist. It seemed fun and didn't require too much real work. That went over well. At the age of nine, I told my parents I wanted to be a dentist.

Wait, Greg, dentists work.

Yes, but I didn't know that then. I had never had a cavity. (I still haven't. Whoo hoo! Toughy Tooth loves me!) My visits to the dentist consisted of a nice lady cleaning my teeth and the dentist looking in my mouth for two minutes, telling me my teeth were great and pointing me to the treasure box for a prize. I thought that was what the dentist did with *all* his patients. It sounded like a pretty good gig to me.

> *Hard work never killed anybody, but why take a chance?*
>
> –Edgar Bergen, actor, comedian

So I guess I was lazy, right? I really just didn't want to work. I was a slacker. That's what I started to believe about myself. The reality, though, was that I wasn't afraid of hard work, I just didn't want to spend my life trapped in a job I couldn't stand.

I spent hours practicing my trumpet. I spent hours more practicing on the basketball team. I spent weeks in the summer building tree houses in the woods behind my house. I mowed lawns to buy my first brand-new bicycle. (I'd had hand-me-down or garage sale bikes until then.) I worked hard when it was something I was passionate about. I thought it would be great to play trumpet in the symphonic orchestra or be the next great NBA player.

I was never drafted into the NBA, and I didn't end up auditioning for the New York Philharmonic, but I was pursuing happiness with a passion when I played basketball and played my trumpet. I was *pursuing* happiness and it was working regardless of the final outcome.

Somehow as I got older I let that powerful, positive focus of *pursuing* happiness and *pursuing* my Passionate Purpose change into something weak and lame. I started just trying to avoid things I didn't like. I started just doing enough to get by.

I was drifting through life. I went to college, because that's what you do in my family when you graduate high school. I did manage to come up with a plan to get a degree in psychology to help people by counseling them, but I'm not sure I was ever truly passionate about it. I never planned to make a lot of money. I thought people who made a lot of money didn't care about people. I was very full of myself for being more compassionate than "the rich."

After earning a degree in psychology from the University of Florida, I quickly realized that I couldn't be a mental health counselor without at least a master's degree. (Maybe I should have been smart enough to figure that out *before* I got the degree. Remember, I made that decision when I was a teenager and knew everything.) Since I couldn't be a counselor without more schooling, the obvious choice was to become a state felony probation and parole officer. Wait, what? Exactly. That decision was based on looking at the want ads in the paper and getting the gig. Not a great way to plan a life, is it? I started out at the princely wage of $18,000 a year.

> *Early to bed and early to rise probably indicates unskilled labor.*
>
> –John Ciardi, poet

There was nothing wrong with this job. I was entering the middle class of America. I was engaged to a beautiful, smart, loving woman and was on my way to "making a living."

But I wasn't pursuing happiness. I could feel a tickling in the back of my brain that something wasn't right. I wasn't reaching to attain my full potential. I wasn't living the life that God wants us to lead. I wasn't making the most of what I had and what I had been given.

I was also stunned by how many people were on parole and how true the adage "close enough for government work" was. One of my duties was to create pre-sentence investigations on the defendants before their court date. I had to interview the individual and do a lengthy background and records check on him to create a score sheet of his previous offenses. My report helped the judge determine the sentence for convicted criminals. I was given a week to do each investigation, although you were given more than one at a time to do. I would often finish these before their due date. As soon as I finished them, I would turn them in. It wasn't long before some of my colleagues told me I needed to slow down. They told me that I was working too hard and making them look bad. I needed to wait to turn in the investigation on the day it was due. More work would be there tomorrow no matter what so I should take it easy. By the way, I wasn't busting my butt. I was just doing my job. I started to figure out if I stayed there long, my attitude would change for the worse and I would get "stuck."

> *The big secret in life is that there is no big secret. Whatever your goal, you can get there if you're willing to work.*
>
> –Oprah Winfrey, talk show host, actress, businesswoman

I read all kinds of self-help books. I listened to motivational tapes. I went back to school and got a master's degree at the University of North Florida in counseling psychology. I began counseling children, adults, and families. I truly enjoyed helping people.

A friend and I even set up an in-home behavior intervention program for a rural county in Florida that had no such offering for its mental health patients. The program was a great success, and I was making double what I made as a felony probation and parole officer. That still may not sound like a lot, but it was a big financial upgrade for me back in 1994. It was my first step to pursue what I thought at the time was my Passionate Purpose.

Those were just a couple of the jobs I worked while trying to find the right vocation. I drifted from job to job searching. I have done everything from working construction and waiting tables to starting my own business as a guest talk show host for shows all across the country. I have been a ropes course instructor and even dug ditches (literally) while waiting to land a job as a mental health counselor.

I hated some of those jobs, but they helped lead me to where I am today. They helped me get to one job I love, being a talk radio host. They even helped me reach my goal of becoming a nationally syndicated talk radio host. They are leading me now into a whole new career of writing, speaking, training, and blogging to help people find their Passionate Purpose and live the lives they've always dreamed about.

To learn all the details of my journey so far, check out the chapter "My Story" near the end of the book.

What Is Your Happiness?

That's kind of a loaded question. There are lots of different types and degrees of happiness. Even when you love your job you still look forward to a vacation. You can really enjoy the company of your extended family, but lose the happy feeling if they come to stay with you for too long. But why not figure out what makes you happy in all aspects of your life and then pursue that happiness?

This isn't as easy as it sounds. I'm talking about finding out what makes you happy and working hard to make that your life. When you find that, you even enjoy the hard work and the *process* of pursuing your Passionate Purpose.

Think about this for a minute: Will you spend more of your life working towards your goals or achieving them? Since most of our time is spent in the process of attaining our goals, doesn't it make sense to strive to enjoy that effort along the way? Won't that help us enjoy our entire lives? How many of us ever do that?

It's All About the Benjamins?

What's the use of happiness? It can't buy you money.

–Henny Youngman

Hey, if your paycheck is big enough you can be happy at any job, right? For a while, that may be true. And I agree that if you aren't earning enough to take care of your family, it's going to be tough to be happy no matter what you're doing. But the money can only take you so far. There are an awful lot of people trying to buy happiness with a bigger paycheck and I think we all know how that ends.

I'm sure you've noticed by now that some of the things you imagined would bring you happiness really didn't. You thought to yourself, "Self, if I could just buy a bigger house, or get that new job, or move to a new city, I would be happy." And then you got the bigger house, or the promotion or whatever, and you were happier for a little while. But the happiness faded quicker than you thought it would. Then you went off in search of the next thing that you thought would make you "happy."

I know that's happened to me quite a few times. It took me longer than I want to admit to learn that a change of scenery, job, or new toy isn't going to make you happy unless you're pursuing what really energizes you.

No matter how much money you make, it won't cover the pain of spending 40-60 hours a week at a job you hate. The golden handcuffs chafe just as much as the cheap ones do.

That doesn't mean money is bad or you have to take a vow of poverty to be happy. I think making a lot of money is a great thing. Creating enough wealth to meet your desires, take care of your family, and give generously to help others is an amazing, worthwhile goal. But making a lot of money at something that makes you miserable just makes you rich and miserable. There are lots of "rich" depressed people on Prozac, getting divorced and struggling with substance abuse. Sound like fun?

Making money at something you love makes you rich and filled with joy. That's a no-brainer, isn't it? When you start pursuing your Passionate Purpose, you're enjoying all the effort you're putting in *and* all the extras that come with it.

One of those extras is happiness. I'm talking about the walking tall, at peace with the world, joy in the core of your being happiness that comes with pursuing your Passionate Purpose.

Don't you want and deserve that happiness and joy that comes from a truly balanced life? Haven't you been searching for it—spiritual, personal, and professional happiness? It's the feeling that you are living up to your potential and God-given purpose in this world.

How many of us ever do the work necessary to discover what that is for us? If we go that far, how many of us continue on to write down our specific goals, create a plan to achieve them, and then work that plan with everything we have? If you choose to do that, you will be in rare air indeed.

Purpose Defined

pur·pose: noun / ˈpərpəs/

1. The reason for which something is done or created or for which something exists.

What do you mean when you use the word "purpose"? Is it your reason for being? Is it why you do that thing you do? Is it one thing that guides everything else? Is it one thing or many? Is it permanent or does it change over time?

What Do You Truly Want?

Your definition of purpose for your life will have an enormous impact on the choices you make, the actions you take, and the goals you accomplish. Just taking the time to define and determine your purpose will irrevocably change your life. Similarly, the default position of never figuring any of this out will also change your course.

> *Cat: Where are you going?*
>
> *Alice: Which way should I go?*
>
> *Cat: That depends on where you are going.*
>
> *Alice: I don't know.*
>
> *Cat: Then it doesn't matter which way you go.*
>
> –Lewis Carroll, *Alice in Wonderland*

For me, purpose means many things. At the macro level it is the reason I was created. It is the point of my existence. It is the prism I use to view everything else I do. If my actions aren't in line with my ultimate purpose, then why am I doing it? Should I be doing it?

However, I believe I have more than one purpose and that those purposes can change over time. At the micro level, I have a purpose in my personal relationships, in my professional life, and in my physical and spiritual lives.

Each one of those purposes changes over time. For example, my purpose in personal relationships is simple and sounds corny. But I like corny. It is:

- To treat every individual I come in contact with the way I would like to be treated
- To look for the best in each person
- To truly listen
- To grow deep connections

Those purposes are slightly different if I'm working on a relationship with my wife, or my father, or my daughters, or a complete stranger. My relationship purpose has changed slightly from when I was a child, to a single adult, to a married man, to a father. It will change again one day when I become a grandfather.

Yes, I have an overarching purpose on relating to people that sustains me through all the changes, but the nuances are important. They help direct me in my daily decisions.

Do You Believe You Have a Purpose?

> *Your purpose in life is to find your purpose and give your whole heart and soul to it.*
>
> —Gautama Buddha, also known as Siddhārtha Gautama, Shakyamuni, or simply the Buddha, on whose teachings Buddhism was founded

I believe everyone has an overarching purpose for their lives. I'm betting you believe that too or you wouldn't be reading this book. Why do we think that? Where did that belief come from? Why do most people think we are on this planet for a purpose? What makes us feel that deep in our souls?

I've asked many different people those questions and I get only slightly different answers.

If you're religious, as I am, you believe your purpose comes from God. You believe that He created you with that purpose in mind and if you seek it, you will find it. As my friend Harold Finch says, "Your purpose is a gift from God. Why would He want to hide it from you? That would be like your dad hiding your birthday present."

If you're not religious, you may still believe that you have a purpose, but you're not sure where it comes from. It may be something that you slowly discover based on your life experiences. Maybe it's just something you create on your own to give your life more meaning. Wherever your purpose comes from, you still agree we all have one.

Then there's the group that doesn't believe in purpose. It really doesn't matter what path they pursue, one is just as good as another.

I don't understand that last group. Do they not feel the daily pull of the question, why am I here? Do they not lie awake at night wondering how they can make a difference, count, or matter? Haven't they ever wanted to jump up from their work cubicle and scream, "I was created for more than this"?

If you're in one of the first two groups, this book is going to help you find your purpose. If you're part of the third group, I'm glad you're reading this. Maybe I can get you to think in a new way, find your purpose, and find new joy and success in life you've never had before.

Find Your Purpose

> *I was seeking comic originality, and fame fell on me as a byproduct.*
>
> –Steve Martin

A Passionate Purpose in your life can lead you to success like you've never experienced before. Your work, your life, and your day shouldn't be something you are trying to "get through." They should be what you're enjoying every day.

There should always be a "Yay in your day."™ Every night I eat dinner with my wife and two daughters and we discuss the Yays in our day. Instead of complaining to each other and reliving all the difficult parts of our days, we focus on the bright spots. This allows us to enjoy those moments and good feelings all over again. Why not focus on feeling good, instead of feeling bad?

We just started discussing a great secret: If you're only going to be happy someday, when you reach whatever goal you're aiming for, then most of the time you won't be happy. But when you're doing something you love, you get to enjoy every step of the journey. The second you *start* pursuing your Passionate Purpose you *become* a success. All the great things that follow are the *results* of the success you have already achieved.

I love that. Steve Martin didn't set out to be famous, or rich, or a celebrity. He set out to do something he loved, being a performer—an original comic. He wanted to entertain people and make them laugh. By pursuing that, all of his "success" followed. By the way, from the time he started doing magic tricks at Disneyland as a teenager until his commercial success, he spent hard years on the road in virtual anonymity. His purpose helped carry him through the difficult times. There were times he wondered what he was doing, but most of the time he was enjoying the process of performing and developing his act. He figured out what he wanted and went after it with everything he had.

If we don't figure out what we want in advance, our journey stinks. We don't have any awesome destination planned so we focus on all the bumps in the road. We become miserable. Or, we end up conforming to what we're expected to do and quite often we take the path of least resistance to an unfulfilling life. We exist, we don't live. We earn a living instead of earning a life. We struggle to get through the day instead of getting greatness out of the day.

When you were a kid what did you want to do as a career when you grew up? Did you want to be a fireman, pro football player, doctor, actor, dancer, or rock star? As you got older, maybe you dreamed of being a CEO, small-business owner, teacher, web designer, nurse, software engineer, lawyer, or author.

Did you ever dream or have the life goal of becoming the assistant to the assistant manager at a job you hate? I don't know anyone who ever wrote that goal down and worked towards it (except maybe Dwight from the TV show *The Office*). How did so many of us look up one day and find ourselves unsatisfied in a life just like that?

We let our dreams and goals fade away. We traded them in for "security," "responsibility," and "reality." We got caught up in the little things of daily life and now every day a little bit of our souls die. (Dude, that is harsh … Sorry.)

If we dare to dream, we're often told we shouldn't go for it because we will fail. Or we're made to feel guilty for wanting an extraordinary life. Maybe you were raised in a family that stressed sacrifice for others at the expense of yourself and you feel ashamed that you want to enjoy your time on this planet.

It's time to change your mindset. Change the tapes, CDs, or MP3s playing in your head. Get those voices saying, "You can't do it," to shut up. Create new MP3s that you can play over and over that support your Passionate Purpose and your goals. If you don't do that, none of this will work.

Instead of telling yourself, "I don't know how to do that," change it to, "I can learn what I need to know in order to do that." Instead of, "Why does this always happen to me?" change it to, "What can I learn from this and how can I change it into something that will help me?" We'll get deeper into how to do this in the chapter on mindset.

If you don't believe you deserve a good life, your subconscious will find a way to sabotage any progress you make. Your brain can't hold two contradictory thoughts at once and be at peace. You can't think you want to pursue your Passionate Purpose *and* think that pursuing your dreams is selfish. You can't strive for success while believing you will never achieve it. You can't focus on your goal of financial wealth while also believing that only greedy people get rich. Eventually, one of those thoughts will take over and crush the other one.

> *No one can serve two masters. Either you will hate the one and love the other, or you will be devoted to the one and despise the other ...*
>
> –Matthew 6:24, NIV

If you are of a divided mind, it's time to ask yourself some questions. Why can't you enjoy what you do *and* live up to your responsibilities? Why can't you help yourself *and* help others? Why can't you become wealthy financially *and* spiritually? Why can't you be a success *and* be a nice person? Who says it has to be one or the other? When will I stop talking in questions?

Stop buying the lie that you can't make any money pursuing your passion. The good news is there is a way.

I'm not saying quit your job, leave your family, and hit the road with your garage band to make it big. (Unless, of course, you're AWESOME! Then just do it, while still taking care of the family, of course.) We all have real responsibilities and we want security for our family. My point is that doing what you are passionate about can be done responsibly and it can eventually give you *greater* security than you have in the job you don't even like or, if we're being honest, may even hate.

The good news is this can happen to you. You can achieve your heart's desire. Do you believe that yet?

Why not *you*?

Most of the successful people in this world are no different than you are. They don't have genius-level intelligence quotients. They didn't graduate from Harvard. They didn't inherit their money. They weren't members of a prestigious country club where all that counts is who you know.

Most successful people in America are of average intelligence, average education, and come from an average family. What sets them apart is that they pursued their passion consistently and never gave up.

Why *not* you?

What Is Your Passionate Purpose?

Have you ever achieved a big dream without trying and without knowing what that dream was? It happens, but it's rare. No one just goes through the motions and becomes super successful. Sam Walton didn't stumble into creating the biggest company in the world. Michael Jordan didn't become the greatest basketball player of all time by just shooting hoops when he was bored. Bill Gates didn't answer an ad in the paper, accidentally create Microsoft and become the richest man on the planet. Martin Luther King Jr. didn't lead the Civil Rights movement because of a coincidence. They found their purpose, their passion, their goals, and they pursued them with everything they had.

But, Greg, I don't know for sure what my Passionate Purpose is. How do I find it? Can I only have one?

I am going to help you with all those questions, starting with a slight contradiction with what I've been telling you. You don't have to know the exact end game of your Passionate Purpose for you to achieve great things and live an extraordinary life.

Great Accidents Can Happen When You Pursue Your Purpose With Passion

Chance favors the prepared mind.

–Louis Pasteur, French chemist and microbiologist

Greg, didn't you just tell me you don't create an extraordinary life by chance? Now you're telling me it can happen by accident? Dude, which is it?

Easy, tiger. Let me explain. Sometimes, as you're pursuing your Passionate Purpose, your goals get bigger than you ever dreamed. It happens more than you think. Sam Walton didn't actually have a goal to become the very biggest retailer. He just kept pursuing his passion and goals for his stores. He kept achieving them and kept going.

You may have heard about the guy who created Post-it® notes. He was actually trying to make a superglue. His “mistake” became a household item.

Have you ever heard of Constantin Fahlberg? He was a chemist in the late 1800s. His life-changing discovery was accidental, and kind of gross. When he went home from work one night he noticed that his wife’s dinner rolls had a special, sweet taste that they hadn’t had before. When she said it wasn’t a new recipe he realized it was something *he* had done. He had been trying to figure out new uses for coal tar. While he was working he got all kinds of residue on his clothes and hands. The residue came off on the dinner rolls and that was what gave them the super sweet taste. (I know. Dude, wash your hands.)

It took another four years of work for Fahlberg to finally patent Saccharin. You see it everywhere in the little pink packets. It’s calorie-free, 300 times sweeter than sugar, and in products from colas to salad dressing. And it all started with an accident.

Sometimes your “mistakes” can save lives.

Wilson Greatbatch was an electrician working on building a device that could record rapid heartbeats. As he was finishing his invention he just needed one more part. He was searching for a 10,000-ohm resistor. When he reached into his box of goodies he accidentally pulled out a 1-mega ohm resistor. (Don’t worry. You don’t need to know the difference between an ohm and an um to get this story.) The device ended up making a 1.8 millisecond pulse. Then it went silent for one second. Then it pulsed again. Essentially, the machine was mimicking a human heartbeat. The pacemaker was born and is now saving lives all around the world.

Sometimes, hard work pays off when you least expect it.

As a kid I loved basketball and baseball. My birthday is in October, and since the leagues were arranged by grade level I was always one of the youngest and smallest guys on the team. I was a pretty good contact hitter on my baseball team, but I wasn’t known for my power. I worked hard at improving my skills and my batting average kept going up.

I finally started growing in my last year of Little League. Just a few games into the season I connected with a fastball and took off running hard. It wasn't until I rounded first that I saw the ball land on the other side of the fence. I was stunned. I had hit a home run? I didn't hit home runs. I never expected to hit a home run. But there it was. I, Greg Knapp, had just hit a home run! I was exploding inside, but tried to act like I'd done it before on the outside. I trotted around the bases in utter bliss.

That was a defining moment in my life. I realized that with hard work I could improve my skills. If I kept at it, I might just surprise myself at how good I could get. I went on to hit 10 home runs that year. Not because I focused on home runs, but because I found joy in the process of pursuing my passion of playing baseball the best that I could.

Greatbatch, Fahlberg, Walton, me, and countless others achieved more than they planned. But it all happened because they were pursuing goals tied to their Passionate Purpose.

Be careful not to get so focused on one way to reach your goal that you miss an amazing opportunity. Always stay open to the chance that something even better than you are aiming for can happen. It just might.

But I'm Not That Smart and I Don't Have All Those Letters After My Name

Sometimes we sell our dream short by talking ourselves down. "I'm not smart enough to do that." "I didn't go to the right school." "I don't have an M.B.A." "You have to be one of the top of your class to be super successful." First of all, telling ourselves those things doesn't help. It hurts the belief and motivation that we need to excel. We're going to work on how to change our self-talk to help us later on in the book. Secondly, those statements just aren't true.

H.J.

H.J. was just an average student. He grew up poor on a farm, but what he really loved to do was to take stuff apart and put it back together. H.J. was so good at it that soon all his neighbors saw him as the go-to guy when they needed something repaired.

But in school he was only a middle-of-the-pack student, and when he turned 16 he decided to drop out. He left home and got work as a machinist's apprentice. After a few years he got married and started running a sawmill. But that wasn't his passion.

H.J. still loved working on machines and anything mechanical. He used that to get a job as an engineer at the Edison Company, where he quickly became chief engineer.

He had started out poor, with a limited education, and was now a "success." That wasn't enough, though. He had a dream of running his own company. It was risky to leave his good paying, stable job, especially with a family to take care of, but he decided to go for it.

He failed. The business went under. He tried again and the business failed again.

This got H.J. thinking. Maybe he didn't have what it took to run his own company. Maybe he should quit. He was 40. It was time to be "responsible." But his drive was strong. This is what he wanted to do with his life. So he tried again.

Third time's the charm, right? Not exactly. His business was not doing well. The investors were worried. They didn't like a strange idea he had of a new way to make his products more efficiently and less expensively. They didn't think it could possibly work. He almost ran out of money. He had to bring in some of the investors as owners to keep things afloat. But then things started clicking. Sales took off. H.J.'s idea worked and he was able to sell his products for a profit at a price that most Americans could afford. He became one of the richest men in the world.

Henry James Ford revolutionized the auto industry, not because he was a genius, or because he had an Ivy League education, or because his parents bankrolled him, or because he knew the right people. He was able to do it because he pursued his Passionate Purpose and never gave up.

What Do You Truly Want?

Failure is simply the opportunity to begin again, this time more intelligently.

–Henry Ford

You may decide you have one purpose and that can guide every phase of your life. Fantastic. Or maybe you see a purpose in some parts of your life, but not in others. Fine. Whatever it is for you, I implore you to figure that out. Why would you want to go on this journey without an idea of where you're going?

Let's go figure it out.

Techniques from the Masters:

- Believe you have a purpose.
- Use what makes you happy as a starting point to discover your Passionate Purpose.
- Define what "Purpose" means in your life.
- Begin to change your mindset: Change the tapes, CDs, or MP3s playing in your head. Get those voices saying, "You can't do it," to shut up. Create new MP3s that you can play over and over that support your Passionate Purpose and your goals.
- Remember: Most successful people in America are of average intelligence, average education, and come from an average family. What sets them apart is that they pursued their passion consistently and never gave up. Why not you?
- Get ready to figure out your Passionate Purpose.

Don't Just Do Something, Sit There!

Your Passionate Purpose Is Already Inside You

If you don't know where you are going, you'll end up someplace else.

–Yogi Berra

OK, Greg, you're getting me fired up. Let's take action right now!

I love where your head is. All the motivation in the world means nothing without action. We're going to get to the action steps to get you to your goal, don't worry. But how can you get to where you want to be when you never get clear on where that is?

Have you heard the story about the world's greatest archer? He was so good that he toured the land challenging all comers to outshoot him. He easily won each contest. It got so boring for him that he started taking people on while blindfolded. Even with the blindfold on he remained undefeated. Finally, a man challenged him by saying, "I can beat you with anyone you pick out of the crowd if you let me set one condition for the match."

The expert archer was so cocky by this time he replied, "I accept your challenge, and I will shoot while wearing a blindfold."

The other man was counting on this. He answered by saying, "My one condition is I get to set up the target wherever I want, *after* you are blindfolded." The archer's heart sank as he realized that no matter how accomplished you are you must know where your target is to have any chance of hitting it.

Let's go find your target.

Turn Inward

Learn to get in touch with the silence within yourself, and know that everything in life has purpose. There are no mistakes, no coincidences, all events are blessings given to us to learn from.

–Elisabeth Kubler-Ross, psychiatrist, author of *On Death and Dying*

The first thing you need to do is schedule time to do some real thinking and soul searching. You are looking to quiet your mind and turn inward.

Have you ever experienced a time when you just knew you should do something? A time when a small, quiet voice in your head told you, "Don't take that job," "Buy that house," "Ask him if he needs help," "Volunteer there," "Pursue being a teacher," "Marry her." That's the voice we're looking for here. (We're *not* looking for the voice that told you to put it all on red at the roulette wheel in Vegas. That's a different voice that you might need to seek professional help for.)

This voice goes by many names. For me, it's the Holy Spirit. For others, it's their conscience, or their inner voice, or the universe, or a higher power. But we've all heard from it at some point in our lives. It's really always there, waiting for us. We have to get quiet enough to hear it. The more you listen for it, the louder and stronger it becomes. The more we ignore it, the harder it is to hear. For most of us, it isn't an audible voice at all. It's a feeling or a thought that pops in our heads. But we tend to know it when we "hear" it.

There were times in my life I pushed it away so hard that I lost it. I thought I knew everything. I was in charge. I didn't need any guidance. I couldn't hear the voice if it was shouting at me because I didn't want to hear it. Those are the times I made some of the dumbest decisions of my life. Have you ever been there? Have you ever heard it?

Don't Just Do Something, Sit There

It's not easy to get quiet enough to hear this voice. In the history of the world we've never had so many distractions. How many minutes a day do you sit quietly and think? For most of us, we rarely if ever do this. After working hard all day, we get busy doing "stuff." We are bombarded by the TV, Internet, email, video games, Facebook, YouTube, Twitter, DVDs, movies, sporting events, texting, smart phones with data plans, Angry Birds, Candy Crush …

My friend Tim limits his son's video game time. When his son goes down to the basement to play his games, he sets a timer. When the alarm goes off on the timer, it's time to turn off the game system. One day his son was playing his games while the rest of the family was upstairs. After a while the timer went off. The alarm is so loud that everyone in the house could hear it—everyone except the boy playing the video games. The alarm kept going, and going, and going. Tim said to his wife, "Let's see how long it takes for him to turn it off."

After five minutes Tim finally went downstairs and said, "Hey, Son, don't you hear the alarm going off?" His truthful response was shocking.

"No, Dad, sorry, I didn't hear it." He was so zoned out with his video game he couldn't hear the blaring alarm five feet away from him. (Of course, if they had called him up for dinner, he would have heard *that*.)

How often are we like that? How many times have we ignored our inner voice when it's trying to help us make the most important choices in our lives? How can we hear it if there is so much noise and junk around us covering it up?

> *Silence is the element in which great things fashion themselves together.*
>
> –Thomas Carlyle, Scottish philosopher, writer

Turn Down the Volume

God's voice is still and quiet and easily buried under an avalanche of clamour.

–Charles Stanley, pastor

We must turn down the volume on everything else if we are truly going to listen for, and hear, our inner voice.

We need to get somewhere with no distractions. Carve out a couple of hours on the weekend or your day off, or whenever works best for you. Pick a quiet, comfortable place. Bring along a notepad and some pens. Now you're ready to work through some exercises that will help you get clear on what you really want.

This is easier than it sounds. We aren't going to look outward and consider every possibility in the universe. That would drive you nuts. You could become overwhelmed and waste years of your life pursuing dead-ends, or become paralyzed and never try anything.

We are going to turn inward and narrow our focus based on who we are, how we were created, and what we already know.

My friend Harold Finch calls this your "personal retreat."

I call this your **"R&R"** time.

It's time to **Remember** and **Rediscover.**

It's time for your **Rebirth.**

Get back to who you are, what you were born to be, and what purpose you are on this earth to pursue. *This* is your life. You weren't created to be ordinary. **Remember** and **Rediscover** what makes you *extraordinary.*

What you are the most passionate about is already in you. To get back to it, just follow your **"R&R"s**.

Remember

Are you ready? Are you in your quiet place with no distractions? Have you turned your phone off? Do you have your **R&R** notebook and something to write with? I have also included some worksheets to walk you through this on my website. You can download them for free at www.gregorybknapp.com

Hey, I see you on the couch. You're not ready to do this. You've decided just to read about it. Maybe you'll do it later. You might even put this book down for a minute to watch a reality show about a "celebrity" having a nervous breakdown because the salon used the wrong nail polish on her manicure and the wrong scent for her aroma massage. Stop! I know taking you through these exercises is harder than just reading the book, but it also has bigger rewards. Isn't that why you started reading this? Plan your retreat now. Don't read any more until you are ready to do this. Start changing your life for the better, *now*, then come back from your retreat and reward yourself with a jumbo bag of Doritos while binge-watching action movies. (Wait, that's not everyone's guilty pleasure? My bad.)

Let's go.

Think back to the times you were the most successful, the most excited, and the happiest about what you were doing. When did time fly for you? When did you feel you were doing what God put you on this planet to do?

Remember the times when people told you, "You were born to do this." Remember the times when you felt like what you were doing was easy for you, even though it wasn't easy for everyone else. These are the times of your life we are searching for. They are the keys to your passion, your joy, and your success.

Write these times down in your **"R&R"** notebook. List as many as you can. **Remember** these times in every aspect of your life—relational, occupational, vocational, spiritual, familial, and physical. You will be surprised what pops into your head if you really get into this.

If you're having trouble, break out your old scrapbooks, your photo galleries, and your Facebook timeline. Use the photos and postings to help relive the best times in your life. Go all the way back to childhood, high school, college, work, play, the early days of your marriage, everything you can remember that brought you joy.

Now pick your favorite memory. **Remember** every detail you can about it. How old were you? Where were you? What were you feeling, seeing, hearing, tasting, and smelling? What was the best part? Take your time. The longer you meditate, pray, and think about it, the more details and memories will come.

Do this with each one of your "best" times. Now take a break. Go for a walk. Get something to eat. Let your mind drift. Don't try to force anything.

How are you feeling? A little drained, but also strangely energized? You are on the right path. Your life is already changing for the better. (And you're one step closer to those Doritos.)

Now, It's Time to Rediscover

You may have forgotten what you used to love to do. Maybe someone told you it was time to give up on that dream and grow up. Maybe they were wrong. Maybe it's time to rediscover that dream.

It's never too late.

Anna

Anna had a talent. It was also something she loved to do. She painted. She drew. She sketched. But she was part of a big family that didn't have much money. There was no time to paint. There certainly wasn't any extra money laying around for painting supplies. So at the age of 12 she started working. For the most part, she put her passion away and focused on more practical things.

She got married, moved to a farm, and started a family. Anna was a hard worker. She made delicious butter and potato chips that sold well. Those profits were used to buy some cows and the family was able to move into dairy farming.

Her life was rewarding and going well, but she still had a strong desire to paint. She dabbled in it, but spent most of her time working hard on the farm.

The years rolled on and she eventually became a widow. She was now in her seventies. It took her sister's repeated suggestions to get Anna to pick up the paintbrush again. Her desire to create art reinvigorated her and by the time she had finished painting she had completed over 1,600 pieces.

Even though it was delayed for decades, Anna Mary Robertson "Grandma" Moses finally followed her Passionate Purpose and it led her to become one of the best-known American painters of all time. We are all richer for her following her dream.

Life is what we make it, always has been, always will be.

–Grandma Moses

Don't cheat the world, and yourself, out of what burns deep inside you. Keep digging it out.

Rediscover

What did you want to be when you were a kid? What did teachers and friends compliment you about? What did you love doing without even caring if you got paid? What dreams and ideas did you bury because you were told they weren't practical and you could never achieve them? **Rediscover** the excitement and wonder you had for your future.

This is brainstorming, anything goes, Fantasyland at Disney time. There are no wrong answers. In your imagination you really can do anything you can dream. Your imagination separates you from everyone else in the world. It is yours alone. Don't allow anyone to squelch it. Breathe new life into it. Nurture it. Rediscover it. Rebirth it. Let it run wild again like it did when you were a child.

If this is starting to sound a bit out there, don't worry. Reality will be back soon enough. There's plenty of time for reality. This ain't it.

Do this exercise again for every aspect of your life—relational, occupational, vocational, spiritual, familial, and physical.

Write them all down in your **"R&R"** book. Now, do the same process we did with our **Remember** exercise. Take each situation and spend some time rediscovering what you loved about it and what you wanted to do before the dream faded away. Get as much detail out of your memories as you can.

It's time for another break. Let your brain kick what you've been **Remembering** and **Rediscovering** around a few times. If you're doing it right, this is hard, mental work. You may have dredged up some painful memories of giving up on the life you wanted. Rest assured that you are right where you need to be right now to turn your life in the direction you want it to go. Everything in your life has led you to this point for you to take action *now*.

The next step is to go back over your Remember and Rediscover lists and see if anything is on both lists. Did you Remember a time when you made easy A's in English class and you Rediscovered a desire from childhood to be a writer? Did you Remember that you always excelled at coordinating group projects and Rediscovered an old desire to be a leader, manager, or business owner?

Rank your favorite memories from your lists. Read them over to yourself. Do any of them make your pulse race a bit when you think about the possibilities? Do you feel an inner nudge when you read one? Does your stomach get the good kind of butterflies that come right before you do something exciting?

My guess is you are experiencing some of those feelings. If you aren't, you need to spend some more time **Remembering** and **Rediscovering**. Come on, admit it. This is more fun than watching that reality show, and it's a lot less fattening than that jumbo bag of Doritos. It's also setting you on the course to your best life.

Your Best Life

Now that you're getting in touch with what you really want, let's go all the way. Spend the next half hour of your limited time on this big, blue marble hurtling through space writing down what your best life would look like. Done correctly, this is an extremely uplifting exercise. Just organizing and prioritizing your best life can increase your happiness, optimism, and belief that you *can* accomplish your goals.

When you answer these questions, remember, we're still in Fantasyland. No limits. What would you do if it were impossible to fail?

What would your career be? What would your marriage be like? What would your income be? How much free time would you have? Where would you live? How many people could you help? What type of relationships would you have with your children? With God? Where would you travel for vacations? How many vacations would you take each year? What would you have crossed off your bucket list? How much would you give away to charity each year? What would your spiritual life be like? Where would you volunteer? How much would you weigh? What would your physical health be? Would you play an instrument, speak a foreign language, or know how to dance? What groups would you belong to? How would you plan out a season of going to every away football game for the Florida Gators? (Wait, sorry, that's one of my dreams again. But that sounds fun, doesn't it? I also need to plan all the best tailgate parties to crash.)

These are just some questions to get you started. What questions do you need to ask yourself to get to your best life?

Time for Your Rebirth

This is your opportunity to make yourself new, to pursue what you know you should do and be. Review your lists from your time creating Your Best Life and from Remembering and Rediscovering and focus on the ones that resonate with you the most. We are going to use these for your rebirth. From these we are going to develop your Passionate Purpose, your goals, and your action plan to reach those goals.

I Just Can't Figure Out What I Want

If you are having difficulty figuring out your Passionate Purpose try the George Costanza method. Remember the *Seinfeld* episode where George figured out that his life was a mess because he always made the wrong choices? He decided he was going to do the opposite of what he would normally do and see how that would work. His life improved greatly! Of course, it wasn't hard to improve the life of a bald, middle-aged, unemployed man who still lived with his parents, but you get the idea.

Give it a try. Figure out all the things you *don't* want in your life. Describe what your worst job would be, who you would work with, what your hours would be, what you would get paid, what your vacations would be like, where you would live, who you would be married to, etc. Detail it as much as you can. Make this your nightmare life. Once you have it all written down, apply the Costanza method. Do the exact opposite. Write down the antithesis of your worst life and you will have your best life.

Your Passionate Purpose

Now is the time to take what you've been working on and write down your Passionate Purpose. It needs to be what *you* care about and what *you* want. It needs to be a deep, burning desire in order to see you through the difficult times that will come.

To get you started, here's my vocational purpose:

> *To inspire people to find and pursue their Passionate Purpose with all they have so they can live out extraordinary lives that will change the world.*

My family purpose:

> *To love, inspire, nurture, serve, give sacrificially, and support my family in pursuing their Passionate Purposes so they can lead the lives they were created for.*

Take some time to write out exactly why you want it. Remember, if you have a big enough "why" you can get through any "how." Your "why" is another way to say your "purpose." When you start with that, everything else falls in line. It is your cornerstone, your lighthouse, your strong shelter, and at times it can be your lifeline. Your strong "why" will help you get through everything life throws at you. If you stay focused on your Passionate Purpose you can still achieve your goals.

You Are Exactly Where You Should Be Right Now

> *The supreme accomplishment is to blur the line between work and play.*
>
> –Arnold Toynbee, British historian, philosopher of history, professor and author

When you really sit down and think about this you will find that you have been preparing for this your whole life. All your experiences, education, relationships, abilities, and work history have set you up to be right here, right now, ready to pursue your Passionate Purpose with reckless abandon. You are exactly where you should be. This is your time. This is the beginning of the extraordinary life you've been dreaming about.

Will Finding My Passionate Purpose Really Help Me?

> *When a man does not know what harbor he is making for, no wind is the right wind.*
>
> –Seneca, Roman philosopher

Greg, this "Passionate Purpose" stuff sounds a little New Agey, touchy-feely to me. I've read some articles and books that are saying the idea of following your passion is a fast way to the poor house. I've even read stuff that says setting goals means you just end up failing and feeling bad about yourself. Is that true?

No, and yes, or yes and no. I'm not trying to avoid answering the question, but that's really the answer. (Those are the answers?) Another great quote from Henry Ford explains it: "If you think you can, or you think you can't, you're right."

Yes, setting goals and not reaching them can be frustrating, and sometimes depressing. You know what can be even *more* depressing? Never setting any goals, never achieving any goals and ending up eating a steady diet of government cheese and living in a van down by the river! (Quick, what TV show?)

You know what's a lot better than not setting goals so you won't feel bad if you don't succeed? Setting goals and actually *achieving* them. You are not going for a passionless existence. You are living an impassioned life!

It's all about your mindset, how you set your goals, the plan you create to achieve them, and the execution of your plan. We are going to go over how to set yourself up for success.

But ask yourself this: What gives you a better chance of living out your dreams, figuring out what they are and pursuing them or just floating through life whichever way the wind blows?

Doesn't Success at Your Job Create Passion?

That works for some people, for a while. But how many people earning a good income do you know who hate their jobs?

Doctors, dentists, and lawyers all make it into the top 20 of highest suicide rates by profession and those are some of our higher-paying jobs. It's not all about the cheddar, is it?

You have to decide these answers for yourself. For me, I want to pursue what I'm passionate about and use that to make me rich in every sense of the word. You might be surprised to find that you will eventually make more money following your passion than you do right now trying to slog through the day. Then again, you might not. But at a certain point, money isn't the number one priority, is it?

My goals definitely include creating a good income for my family and me, but a goal like earning $1 million per year is not my primary motivator. It's not my top "why" for my Passionate Purpose. My "whys" include inspiring people, creating more freedom for myself, helping people live their dreams, a flexible schedule, doing what I love, and taking more vacations with my family. If you took all those away and simply paid me more for doing a soul-sucking job 50 hours a week, I'd say no thanks.

There are countless “hows” to make money, but if your Passionate Purpose isn’t the “why” behind your “how” you are on the path to burnout and apathy regardless of your income.

How about you? How is doing a job just for the money working out for you?

Techniques from the Masters:

- Turn inward and turn down the volume to do your R&R. Carve out a couple of hours on the weekend or your day off, or whenever works best for you. Pick a quiet, comfortable place. Get clear on what you really want.
- **Remember** your best days. Write down the times you were the most successful, the most excited, and the happiest about what you were doing. Get the free worksheets at www.gregorybknapp.com
- **Rediscover** the excitement and wonder you had for your future. What did you want to be when you were a kid? What did teachers and friends compliment you about? What did you love doing without even caring if you got paid? What dreams and ideas did you bury because you were told they weren't practical and you could never achieve them? Write the answers down.
- Compare your R&R notes and pay special attention to the items that show up on both lists.
- Write out what your best life would look like. No limits. Fantasyland time.
- **Rebirth**: This is your opportunity to make yourself new, to pursue what you know you should do and be. Review your lists from your time creating Your Best Life, and from Remembering and Rediscovering and focus on the ones that resonate with you the most.
- Write down your Passionate Purpose. It needs to be what *you* care about and what *you* want. It needs to be a deep, burning desire.

Goals

How to Create Goals That Will Lead You to
Where You Want to Go in Record Time

The Quickest Way Between Two Points Is a Goal

My goal is to have such an awesome life that only Morgan Freeman should narrate the movie about it.

–Anonymous

I know goal setting works. I've seen people set and meet goals they originally thought they could never achieve. Setting goals helped me go from having no education, training, or experience in radio to becoming a nationally syndicated radio talk show host in just nine years. I've read countless stories about real people using goals to change their lives for the better. I am convinced there is no faster way to get where you want to be than with specific, measurable goals that you take consistent action on.

People tend to have one of two opinions on goal setting.

You either think: "Goals don't work. They're psychobabble nonsense. Setting goals and not reaching them just demoralizes you and makes you less motivated to do anything."

Or you think: "Setting goals will help get you to where you want to be quicker than you ever thought possible."

Which is correct? Both.

Um, Greg, I don't think you understand the question. That isn't a "both"-type situation. Two words for you, "mutually exclusive," like Hugh Hefner and monogamy. Like Donald Trump and a good hair day. Like *Jersey Shore* and class.

Not true. The answer is "both" because it depends on you. If you believe setting goals works or if you believe setting goals doesn't work, you're right … for you.

Setting a goal works, but it's not a Ronco rotisserie oven. You can't just "set it and forget it."

Most of the people who create a goal never follow through and take the action necessary to make the goal a reality. So they believe goals don't work and they're right—for them.

The super achievers, the Goaldiers who take consistent action on their goals and achieve them, believe goals work and they're right—for them. (Goaldiers, you know, like soldiers. Too corny? I kinda like it. It's growing on me.)

Which one will you be?

What's Your Why?

> *If people knew how hard I worked to get my mastery, it wouldn't seem so wonderful after all.*
>
> –Michelangelo

Now that you have found your Passionate Purpose, the other big question is, why do you want it? Every successful person I know agrees with the idea that if your "why" is strong enough, you will do what is necessary to find the "how." Then you will put in the work to make it happen. And there will be plenty of work. You must make yourself the person you need to be to achieve your goals. You must be committed to increasing your education, skills, and experience to meet the demands that come with what you want. Figure out what they are and do something every day to get you closer to where you want to go.

There is a caveat to your why. You need to come to terms with what you're willing to give up to reach your goals. You will have to give up some things to get there. To stay in balance and live the life of character you want to live you also have to decide right now what you're *not* willing to give up. For example, if you have to give up so much of your time and attention for your goal that it would lead to divorce and no time with your children, I hope that's giving up too much for you.

What do I mean when I say you will have to give up a lot to achieve your goals? Have you ever marveled at a concert pianist, guitar god, or professional athlete? Wouldn't you love their skill? I once heard of a woman who attended a beautiful piano concert. Afterwards she had the opportunity to speak with the musician. She gushed with her praise and said, "I would give anything to play like you do." Without missing a beat the pianist replied, "No, you wouldn't." The woman assured her she would. With a knowing sigh, the musician said, "Are you willing to spend the next 25 years of your life practicing the piano for five to seven hours a day? Are you willing to have people push you like you've never been pushed before? Are you ready to live in seedy apartments and play awful venues until you truly make it? Because that's what it took for me to play like I do today." The other woman excused herself and went back to the bar.

If this sounds like a lot of hard work, it is. It's a lot easier to come home tired from work, eat dinner, pop a top, click on the TV and turn off your brain. Hey, sometimes we all need to do that. But if you want to pursue your Passionate Purpose you are going to have to do things others *won't* so you can eventually do what others *can't*.

> *Do what others won't, so later you can do what others can't. That's how you pursue your Passionate Purpose and live an extraordinary life.*
>
> –Greg Knapp

Pursuing your Passionate Purpose is not a get-rich-quick scheme. It requires a lot of you. But if you take the time to change your mindset, overcome the fears holding you back, educate yourself where needed to meet your goals, find a big enough "why" to keep you motivated, find some "hows" you are passionate about, and pursue it with everything you have, you will stop trying to make a living and instead make a life. Isn't that worth it?

Remember the Declaration of Independence says, "… all men are created equal, that they are endowed by their Creator with certain unalienable Rights, that among these are Life, Liberty and the *pursuit* of Happiness."

Enjoy the *pursuit* …

> *If our country is worth dying for in time of war let us resolve that it is truly worth living for in time of peace.*
>
> –Hamilton Fish, American statesman and politician

Set Your Goals

> *You can do anything, but you can't do everything.*
>
> –David Allen, productivity consultant, author

Successful people determine their Passionate Purpose, set specific, measurable goals with deadlines, and then take action.

Your Passionate Purpose is not the same thing as a goal. It's basically your mission statement for your life. From this you will create your main goal and then develop all your secondary goals. However, you have to be careful not to create so many goals that you lose focus and become overwhelmed to the point that you don't achieve anything.

This isn't about creating the "perfect" goal. You can drive yourself crazy doing that. Your goals will change as you go about achieving them, but your primary Passionate Purpose probably won't. Think of this process as laying out one path you can go down while living your impassioned life. Always allow for something even better to come along.

Setting a goal is like deciding where you want to go on a trip. You have to decide where you are going to get there, but if that's all you do you're still sitting at home. You have to actually get the map, plot your course, get in the car, and drive the proper route until you get there. Sometimes (guys) you even have to stop for a second to ask for directions.

OK, you could just punch the address into the GPS and follow the instructions, but you get my point. In fact, the GPS idea isn't always so great. Sometimes it takes you the long way. Sometimes it tries to take you through a lake. Some people have followed the GPS until they get stuck in the middle of nowhere and they have to call 911 for help.

Even if you make the right decision on where to go, get the best map, and make the best plan you will still have problems. You might get a flat, or run out of gas, or take a wrong turn. That annoying lady on the GPS might have to say "recalculating" 100 times. But as long as you keep focused on your destination, readjusting your plan to handle the obstacles, and never give up, you will get there.

Right about now you might find yourself saying, "Greg, that's like really hard and I'm busy and I'm tired and it's Shark Week on Discovery Channel. If it's my dream it should be easy, shouldn't it? Haven't you heard that if you love what you do you never work another day of your life? You just helped me find my Passionate Purpose, isn't it all easy peasy from here?"

That sounds great. Especially when you're sitting in your cubicle recovering from the last all-staff meeting where you learned how to fill out your TPS report in triplicate and you're dreaming about using a line from a country song to drop the "I quit" bomb on your boss who thinks fart humor is high comedy.

Yes, following your Passionate Purpose will be rewarding, fulfilling, and fun. But the reality is even if you love your work, it's still work.

Ask Michael Jordan if he worked to become a great basketball player. Ask Bill Gates if he worked to build Microsoft. Ask Yo Yo Ma if he worked to learn to play the cello. (And ask him how he got that name Yo Yo Ma. That's a cello player with crazy street cred.)

Now, if you are doing something you're passionate about and your why for doing it is compelling, the hard work won't feel as hard. Sometimes you will even get into the zone or the flow, or whatever you want to call it, where time flies and you feel like everything is going right. That's part of the goal as well.

But here's some truth. It's hard to change your life. It's hard to follow your dreams. It's scary. It can be risky. You will fail at times. You will get discouraged. Life will get in the way. But it's *worth* it.

Do you remember learning to ride your bike? My older brother taught me. We lived on a hilly street. My brother had me get on the bike at the top of the hill. He would run alongside me holding the bike and we would stop in our driveway. Then we'd walk the bike back to the top of the hill and start the whole process again. I started getting pretty good. I was even pedaling now. The next time down the hill I was feeling great, I was really moving. I turned into my driveway and was hurtling toward the closed garage door. I yelled to my brother, "Dave, stop. Stop! Dave, stop!" Bam! I crashed right into the garage door. My brother thought I was doing so well he could let go of the bike and quit running beside me. The problem with that was he didn't tell me and didn't teach me how to stop. Whoops.

It hurt. This was back in the day when kids didn't wear helmets, and I had a big lump on my head. But I didn't say, "Well that bike riding stuff hurts. I'm never doing that again." I wanted to ride a big-boy bike without training wheels. I wanted the freedom that came with that. I wanted to keep up with the older kids in the neighborhood. I put my football helmet on and got back on my bike.

You might not have a brother who rammed you into a closed garage door, but I bet you fell a few times learning to ride your bike. I also bet that didn't stop you from learning to ride. Why would you risk getting hurt again? Why not give up? Because we all know that some things are worth the pain.

Author Ken Davis puts it this way, "You will fall. It will hurt. It will be worth it." As you pursue your Passionate Purpose there will be times when you fall, there will be times when it hurts, but if you persevere it will be worth it.

With all the work I've done in inspiration, motivation, and self-improvement, I thought I could write this book in six months. Guess what? It took three years!

Regular life slowed me down. I had to go to my regular job. I wanted to spend time with my family. I got sick. I got tired. I even got sick *and* tired. I watched some football games and movies. I lost my motivation for a while. I lost focus. I questioned if I had anything new or worthwhile to say. I wrote multiple drafts, improving it each time.

But here's the key: I never gave up. I rewrote my goals when I stumbled. I came up with new action plans on what I would do every day in order to complete my book. I had a "why" that was big enough to carry me through all my fears and all the stuff that got in my way. You can do the same thing.

Remember, when you're working on your Passionate Purpose and pursuing your worthy goal you are already a success. The process becomes part of the fun. You are enjoying life *now*—not 10, 20, or 30 years from now when you retire. In fact, when you are following your Passionate Purpose you may not ever *want* to retire. But if you aren't working on the right goals and enjoying the work it takes to get there, it can become a miserable life. That's true even if you're making a good income and living the life everyone else thinks you should be leading.

> *When you dance, your purpose is not to get to a certain place on the floor. It's to enjoy each step along the way.*
>
> –Wayne Dyer, self-help author and motivational speaker

Time for Action

Now that you're starting to get a handle on what you really want out of life, it's time to amp things up. It's time for you to get aggressive on what you want, time to attack it like you're in the Army. It's time to become a "Goaldier." (Is it growing on you yet?)

OK, Goaldiers, it's GOAL time! Let's get Goaling. Be a Goal-getter. Get up and Goal. (OK, I'm done.)

Write Your Goals Down

> *A dream is just a dream. A goal is a dream with a plan and a deadline.*
>
> –Harvey Mackay, businessman, author

I've been studying how to create and achieve goals for over twenty years. I've learned a lot from some of the best experts in the field like Brian Tracy, Zig Ziglar, Steven Covey, Tony Robbins, and Jack Canfield. These techniques work.

You may have heard about the Harvard study on goal setting. It found that only three percent of a graduating class wrote down specific goals. Ten years later, those three percenters were earning 10 times as much as the rest of the class. Cool story, bro, but not true. It turned out to be an urban myth. But there is quite a bit of research that shows goal setting *does* work, if you do it the right way.

Dr. Gail Matthews, Ph.D. of Dominican University in California, did a study where she randomly assigned her subjects to five different groups. She wrote a summary of the set up of her research:

"Participants in Group 1 were simply asked to think about their goals (what they wanted to accomplish over the next four weeks) and then asked to rate that goal on the following dimensions: Difficulty, Importance, the extent to which they had the Skills and Resources to accomplish the goal, their Commitment and Motivation to the goal, whether or not they had Pursued this goal before, and if so their Prior Success.

Participants in Groups 2-5 were asked to write (type into the online survey) their goals and then to rate their goals on the same dimensions.

Group 3 was also asked to formulate action commitments.

Group 4 was asked to formulate action commitments and send their goals and action commitments to a supportive friend.

Group 5 was asked to formulate action commitments and send their goals, action commitments, and weekly progress reports to a supportive friend. Participants in this group were also sent weekly reminders to email quick progress reports to their friend."

The results:

Group 1 had a 43 percent success rate of accomplishing their goals on time. Look how powerful it is to just *think* about your goals, skills, and motivation level. That's a great start. But the study showed you can amp that success rate way up with a little more planning and action.

Group 5 had a 76 percent success rate of accomplishing their goals on time. When you think about your goals, write them down, formulate an action plan, declare it publicly, and share weekly updates with a supportive friend, your odds of success soar. Each one of those actions was found to significantly increase your rate of accomplishment.

Sharpen Your Pencil

If your goal isn't written down, it's really just a daydream.

Write down your goals. There's something almost magical about writing your goals down. Writing helps you organize and prioritize your thoughts. It helps you filter out the fluff and get serious. It helps make your goals real to you in a way that just thinking about them can't.

As you start writing your goals down make sure they fit your Passionate Purpose, your why. The whole point is to get your life focused on your why. These written goals are not ends in themselves, they are measurable ways to show you're on the right track pursuing your Passionate Purpose.

Here's what I mean. What is the purpose of your financial goal? Yes, of course it's to earn more money, but why? What is your purpose for earning more money? Is it so you can take better care of your family, make memories with them on special vacations, allow your children to take piano lessons, expand your business so you can positively affect more people, give more generously? What is it about the goal that pushes your Passionate Purpose forward?

It's All in the Details

Every goal you create must be:

- Specific and definite
- Measurable
- Stated in the present tense as if you already have it
- Positive
- With a deadline
- Open to something even better that you might not have thought of

Be Specific

Generalities are killers. They will sap the energy right out of your goal.

Not this: "I will make more money."

This: "I am earning _______ per year."

Not this: "I will attain a healthy weight."

This: "I am maintaining the healthy weight of 165 pounds."

Make it Measurable

If you can't measure it, how do you know you truly achieved it? How will you even know when you're moving in the right direction?

Not this: "I will improve my guitar playing."

This: "I am able to play 'Stairway to Heaven' in tempo with no mistakes.

State It in the Present Tense

Your subconscious responds best to the present tense. There should be no doubt that you are going to reach your goal. So write it, think about it, and talk about it as if you already have it.

Not this: "I will become salesman of the month."

This: "I am salesman of the month for December."

Positive

The unconscious mind doesn't understand negative commands. The conscious mind doesn't do so well with them either. Quick—DON'T think about a flying purple elephant. Hey, I told you NOT to think about it. It's impossible now, isn't it? That's how our brain works. So phrase your goal in the positive. Your mind responds positively to what you think about all day long. It doesn't care what you put in it. It will focus on something you don't want as hard as what you do want. Therefore, you must train yourself to think of your *positive* goals. Unleash the unlimited power of your mind to work for you 24/7. It even works when you're asleep.

Not this: "I will stop getting to work late." (This will have you focusing on getting to work late, exactly what you *don't* want.)

This: “I am arriving at work on time, feeling refreshed and ready to achieve.”

Give Yourself a Deadline

The right type of pressure makes diamonds. We are going to put the right kind of pressure on ourselves. How long do you think it should take you to reach your goal? Be realistic. You don’t want to set a crazy deadline, miss it, and then feel like you blew it. That can lead to you coming to the erroneous conclusion that the whole idea was stupid. Figure out how long it should take and then set the deadline.

If you’re looking to lose weight, most people can lose 1-3 pounds a week. So if you’re looking to lose 15 pounds, pick between 5-15 weeks to get it done.

Not this: “I am the healthy weight of 165 pounds.”

This: “I am maintaining the healthy weight of 165 pounds on Dec. 22.”

Or Something Even Better

As we discussed earlier, don’t limit yourself with your goals. What if you aim for the sun but get the stars too? Would that be OK? I love how Jack Canfield puts it. Always leave open the possibility of exceeding your goals. End every written goal with the words, “or something even better.”

That includes even changing your mind about your goals. As you get more information and experience you might tweak what it is you truly want. Whatever it is, just keep tweaking and don’t give up.

Not this: “I am earning __________ per year on Dec. 22.”

This: “I am earning ___________ per year on Dec. 22, or something even better.”

Two Caveats

1) Don't spread yourself too thin.

Did you really dig deep and come up with some great goals? How many? Be careful. There are only so many goals you can focus on and achieve at the same time. I recommend prioritizing your goals and starting on the one that will change your life the most.

Jay Papasan and Gary W. Keller have some great advice on this in their book, *The ONE Thing.* When you focus on the ONE Thing, you will be surprised how much progress you can make in a short time. Then you can take that success and build on it. Just don't spread yourself so thin trying to chase ten goals that you miss them all. This idea runs right into caveat #2.

2) Be realistic, but go big.

That's contradictory advice, isn't it? Well, we want to dream big. We want to stretch ourselves and even have unrealistic goals. However, we want to set ourselves up for success, not for failure. If you've never run a business in your life, setting the goal to create the next Apple or Coca-Cola with one billion in earnings one year from now might be setting yourself up for a big disappointment. You can keep that as your ultimate goal, but set up the mini-goals to get there over time.

Start small and *then* go BIG!

Have your BIG goal, but start with a small goal that you feel pretty sure you can achieve. That can start you on the way to your BIG goal. The more small successes you pile up, the more your confidence grows and the better your chances become that you will reach goals you never thought possible.

As you reach these mini-goals the confidence in your conscious and subconscious mind will increase exponentially. Now it's time to really dream big. The only way to expand your thinking of what's possible and to change your mindset to believe that you can actually achieve what you want is to take off all limits. Be unreasonable! Be unrealistic! Be unusual! Who wants to live an average, normal life?

OK, Greg, I've heard this before. If you can conceive it and believe it, you can achieve it. Yada, yada, yada, blah, blah, blah. I'm 60 years old. No matter how much I believe I can be an NFL quarterback, it ain't gonna happen.

You got me. You're right. So I guess it's time to stop pursuing any goal. Especially any goal that sounds unreasonable. Sounds like you've got a fun life ahead. Good luck!

The scenario you painted is sad. Yes, there are some dreams we can't achieve, but how does that kind of thinking help you? If you really wanted to be an NFL quarterback and you are now too old to do it, what could you do that still fits the Passionate Purpose behind that desire? Would coaching football fit? How about becoming a referee for high school football games? Maybe you could work for a college or pro team in some capacity. Why do you have to give up your Passionate Purpose because one door is closed to it?

I'll tell you this. You may not be able to achieve it just because you believe it. But I don't see too many people out there achieving things they *don't* believe. Do you?

Many of us have had people tell us we can't do the things we really want to do. We've been told to stop dreaming and be "realistic." We've been told we will never achieve the desires we have deep in our hearts. It's time to destroy those negative tapes or MP3s playing in our heads and replace them with the biggest cheerleader you can imagine. Other than God, there is no power greater than the human mind focused on a Passionate Purpose.

Once you begin reaching every goal you set, why not try the big ones? You will start to believe you can accomplish anything. Guess what? You can!

OK, I Have a Goal, Now What?

Have you ever created the perfect goal and then nothing happens? You don't know how to make it a reality. You don't even know where to start.

To make it a reachable goal you need to take it and develop a plan to get from where you are to where you want to be. Here's how you can do it.

Focus on your goal. Spend time thinking about it throughout your day. You've heard this before. It's not new, but it works. Put your written goal that you just finished creating on an index card, your smart phone, or something else that you can carry around all the time. Read your goal in the morning, at lunch, and before you go to bed. Ruminate on it.

This isn't because you're just hoping that your goal will come true. It's to fire up your brain cells to work on solutions to your goal. It's to keep you focused on the work necessary to succeed.

As Earl Nightingale says, you become what you think about. The more you think about your goal the more you become the success you want. There is something powerful about the human mind focused on a Passionate Purpose. Once you discover this, your life will change forever.

When I got my start in radio I was thinking about it all the time. How would I break in? What would make my show entertaining and informative? Why would people want to tune in to hear what I had to say? How would I learn to become a radio pro? How could I become nationally syndicated? I wrote down and thought about my radio goals every day.

Almost magically, answers to all my questions started popping into my head. Some of the answers were things I knew but had forgotten. Others were about how to research what I needed to know, or whom I could talk to in order to get the next bit of information I needed to move forward. The most important thing I figured out was that I had to take action. Even though I didn't have a fully baked plan, I knew the next step I needed to take. I took it and a funny thing happened. The *next* step I needed to take appeared.

I got my start in radio in a very strange way. I had no education, training, or experience in broadcasting. I was simply a fan of talk radio and I had a great desire to become a talk show host. I had no idea how to even get started in the radio business. The idea of hosting my own show seemed like a fantasy. But I wanted it so bad, I finally took action.

I called the top station in town and gave them my pitch: "I really want to get into radio. Is there anything I can do for you to get my foot in the door?" The response from the program director was the best lesson on taking action I have ever had. He said, "Can you be here by five o' clock?"

That started my radio career. If I had waited for the perfect time, or until I had gotten a broadcasting degree, or I had met the right people, or whatever excuses I kept making for myself, I would never have become a radio talk show host. Now, when I showed up at five I wasn't put on the air. I did nighttime grunt work and producing, but it got me in the business and led me to my radio dreams. Whatever your dreams are, you can do it too. Take action.

Have you ever awoken with an idea on how to solve that problem you've been working on? Maybe while you're washing the shampoo out of your hair or jogging that last mile back home, all of a sudden inspiration hits. That's the power of your subconscious mind. We are tapping into that and putting it on steroids by focusing on your goal all day long.

As you concentrate on this goal and think about it day after day, you will be amazed at how many ideas on how to achieve your goal "just come to you." Don't let even one of these ideas slip away. Use the recorder on your smart phone to make an audio note to yourself. Keep a notepad by your bed for that crazy thought that comes in the middle of the night. It's all grist for the mill. (Be careful on the whole "middle of the night" thing. You may wake up and find you made an extremely important, life changing, awesome note to yourself that says: Don't forget to axrtgnt snurgltop! Yes, writing when you're half asleep can be hazardous to your success.) Read over these ideas every night after you read your goals. You will be shocked at how many great ideas are inside you.

You also want to spend time researching your goal. How have other people done it? Are there books on it? Will a Google search turn up some ideas? Do you know anyone who is where you want to be? Can you take them to lunch and pick their brain? Might they be willing to be your mentor if you can do something to help them? Don't be afraid to ask. Most people love helping others, especially when they are the expert and you sincerely want their assistance.

Due Diligence

You also need to do your due diligence on your Passionate Purpose and your goals. What price are you willing to pay to go on this journey? What price would be too high? What are you not willing to give up for it? Does this dream truly resonate with you? Is it your dream or are you doing this to please someone else? Are you able to take care of yourself and your family while pursuing this? Are there other people who are earning a good income doing what you are looking to do?

In other words, after all the dreaming, spend some time back in the real world and start figuring out how this could really work. It would be tragically sad to pursue your Passionate Purpose for years only to find out nobody wants or needs what you're trying to do.

Mini-Goals and Daily Actions

You have your main goal and you have a list of ideas on how to pursue it. What's next? It's easy to get into a paralysis by analysis phase right about now. There's so much to do to reach your goal, you don't know how to get started. As we talked about earlier, it's time to start small and go BIG.

Break your big goal into a series of mini-goals. You should have daily, weekly, monthly, and yearly mini-goals and deadlines leading you to your BIG goal. Don't let a day go by without doing *something* to further your Passionate Purpose.

Let's suppose you need to lose weight. Your goal might be, "I am maintaining my healthy weight of 165 pounds on Jan. 15, or something even better."

You write down a bunch of ways to reach this goal:

- Eat between 1,700 and 1,900 calories a day. (The exact amount depends on your current caloric intake, exercise level, and your biology.)
- Eat six servings of vegetables a day.
- Jog every other day.
- Lift weights three times a week.

- Join a basketball league.
- Work out with a friend.
- Stop eating potato chips and ice cream.
- Only drink beer on the weekends.

Now pick out the ideas you like the best that you believe you can do consistently.

For example:

Eat between 1,700 and 1,900 calories a day spread out over five meals, jog every other day, and lift weights three times a week.

Now make your plan.

You currently eat 2,300 calories a day, you don't exercise at all, and you weigh 195 pounds. Doctors say you can safely lose three pounds a week. Let's go easy at first and aim for two pounds a week. That means we should reach our goal in 15 weeks on January 15. Create goals for your weight for each of the 15 weeks.

Now create daily goals for your exercise and for your diet.

For example:

- Day 1) Buy running shoes. Research how to begin a jogging program.
- Day 2) Create healthy menus for the week. Research weightlifting.
- Day 3) Jog/walk for 10 minutes. (It's your first day and you don't want to go too hard too fast and give up.) Begin eating from your healthy menus.
- Day 4) Begin your weightlifting program.
- Day 5) Continue your jogging program.

Are you starting to see how we do this? I've left out how detailed you can get, but I think you have the picture now. If we keep this up every day we will reach our 15-week goal. Celebrate each week as you lose another two pounds. You are on your way.

No matter what your goal is, use the same process. Start with your main goal, create mini goals to get there, and take action every day, week, month, and year to get where you want to go.

Share and Work on Your Goal with a Friend

If you really want to ramp up the odds you will succeed, find a supportive friend to work with. Find someone who shares a similar goal and make a pact to encourage each other. Meet in person, email, or text each other at least once a week to check each other's progress. You will be pleasantly surprised at the positive pressure this puts on you to stay focused on your goal and follow through on your plan of action.

It's a lot easier to slack off your daily actions towards your goal when nobody else will even know. You will get tired. You will have days were your motivation lags. Daily life will whisper to you that skipping one day won't really matter. One day will become two and then it will become skipping more days than working. A partner can help you resist that.

When you know you are going to meet with your friend in four days and have to admit that you really didn't pursue your Passionate Purpose this week, you will have an added incentive to keep moving forward. You have the positive pressure to help yourself and to help your friend by keeping him on target as well.

What Happens if I Miss the Deadline on My Goal?

Give yourself some grace. Sometimes you will stumble. But you fail at 100 percent of the goals you never strive for. Celebrate your successes. Celebrate your failures, too. They show you are trying for something more than average. Learn from failure. Use those lessons to improve and start piling up successes. Repeat the cycle. If you are truly pursuing your Passionate Purpose, you can even enjoy what you learn and do when things don't work out exactly the way you wanted them to.

If you never give up, you never truly fail. You *will* achieve your goals.

Remember to Focus

Most people have more than one goal they are aiming for. That's fine, but be careful. If you have too many plates up in the air at the same time, you're eventually going to start dropping them. The more focused you can stay on a goal, the quicker you will reach it. There are only 24 hours in the day, stay focused and use them wisely.

Motivation Doesn't Last So Why Bother?

Maybe you've tried this before, got motivated, had some initial success, and then gave up—what happened? Did you start to think that all this personal development stuff doesn't work? Maybe you decided that getting motivated isn't worth it because it just wears off after a while.

Let me ask you something. Did you eat more than once today? I guess that eating thing wears off. Did you take more than one shower this week? I guess that whole bathing thing wears off.

Yes, virtually everything wears off if we let it. I used to know how to do calculus problems. It's been 27 years since I've done one and I couldn't do one right now if my life depended on it. It wore off.

Did you exercise at the gym one day and say now you're fit for the rest of your life? Ridiculous, right? Then why do we think that we only have to be motivated once and we're set for life? Why do we think there's some easy button to success and to pursuing our dreams?

We will get there, but it takes deliberate, persistent effort aimed at our Passionate Purpose. It takes improving ourselves day after day to become the person we want to be.

> *Remember, it's not what you hear or read that changes you, it's what you* do *with what you hear and read.*

I would love to be one of the people who tell you that if you have passion and desire and you think positive thoughts your dream will appear at the end of a double rainbow with pots of gold and butterflies and sprinkles on Twinkies that have no calories—but that's not the truth.

That belief system won't get you where you want to be. It could actually take you farther from your goals. Without a strategy and daily action on your goals, your results will probably be disappointing, if not nonexistent. That could demoralize you to the point of giving up. Not exactly what we're looking for.

Setting goals works. But you need to get clear on *what* you want, *why* you want it, that you *have* to achieve it, *when* you will reach it, and *how* you'll do it. Then you must *take consistent action* to get it done.

Oh, that's all? Sweet! Then I'll create world peace for breakfast and save the whales after lunch.

I know it can sound intimidating and overwhelming, but when you do this one step at a time it's really not that hard. You already know how to do everything we're going to do. Just like with your Passionate Purpose, your goals and the way to reach them are already inside of you. I'm going to help you pull them out.

Inspiration v. Motivation

It may sound like word games, but I believe there is a difference between motivation and inspiration. My purpose isn't just to motivate you for a short time. My purpose is to help inspire you to find your Passionate Purpose. When you find and pursue that you will become self-motivated.

You will still have ups and down on how motivated you are. But when you find your why you have a reservoir of motivation in your soul that you can draw from whenever you need it.

Stay Committed to Your Purpose

There is a reason we started by finding your Passionate Purpose. The best way to overcome all obstacles in your journey is to have a great Passionate Purpose for what you are doing. If your only purpose is to make money, you probably won't make it. Why are you really doing this? If the "why" is great enough, you will get through any "how" or "what." Every time you hit a wall, refocus on your why.

Man is only great when he acts from passion.

–Benjamin Disraeli, two-time British prime minister and author

You're So Close

Know this: You are now in an elite group of people walking this planet. You have defined your Passionate Purpose, created goals and mini-goals for your success, and developed an action plan to get you there. Most people never do this in their entire lives. You are on your way to a totally new life! If …

Yup, there is a HUGE "if." If you stop now, this will all be a complete waste of time. In fact, if you stop now, all this might actually hurt you instead of help you. You might start to believe that none of this really works. It's all nonsense and a waste of time. You are not in control of your own destiny. You will never live the life of your dreams. At best, you are doomed to a life of mediocrity.

Quick! Hide all the sharp objects in your home! Life is no longer worth living!

See how ridiculous that line of "reasoning" can go? Is that really how you want to look at the world and your power over your own life? I can tell you that the most successful people do not allow themselves to think that way. From now on neither will you.

Instead, you are going to keep a positive focus on your goal and take daily action on your plan.

Go!

You must take action. Without action, all of this is just a lot of time and effort wasted. Without action you will lose focus, become frustrated, decide goal setting doesn't work, and quit. So here's my advice: Don't wait one day, *start now*. If you put this off until you're "ready," or your busy project at work ends, or until after your vacation, or until the kids are grown, or the time is right, or (fill in the excuse) you will never start or finish. If you only remember one thing from this book, remember this:

Go!

You might not feel sure how to do all this. It may seem overwhelming. That's OK. Go anyway.

When you drive to work do you wait until all the lights turn green before you start driving? No, you plot your course and then you start driving. You drive until you hit a red light and stop for a moment until the light turns green. Then you go as far and as fast as you can until you hit the next red light, stop for a moment, and then you get going again. You continue like that until you reach your destination.

That's how this works, too. Once you start moving you will be amazed how much the world lines up for you. Have a little faith and watch what happens.

Martin Luther King Jr. put it this way:

> *Faith is taking the first step even when you don't see the whole staircase.*

As soon as you "Go!" and start taking action on your Passionate Purpose, you are a success. The staircase will start appearing faster and faster. This is why you are here. The possibilities are endless for your life now. You aren't just surviving, you are *thriving*. You aren't just earning a living, you're earning a *life*.

Go!

Techniques from the Masters:

- Create your main goal from your Passionate Purpose. All your secondary goals will come from this.
- Write your goals down. Every goal you create must be: Specific, Definite, Measurable, Stated in the present tense, Positive, with a Deadline, and Open to something even better.
- Don't spread yourself too thin. It's great to have more than one goal, but if you chase too many rabbits you will catch none.
- Be realistic for now. Start small, succeed, and then go BIG.
- Break your big goal into mini-goals.
- Write down your daily, weekly, monthly, and yearly action plans.
- Do *something* every day in pursuit of your goals.
- Reward yourself for every success.
- Go!

You Think, Therefore You Do, Therefore You Are

You become what you think about.

–Earl Nightingale, radio host, motivational speaker, and author

Take a look around you right now. What do you see? A couch, a chair, walls, furniture, lights, windows? If you're in your car and listening to the audio version of this book, what do you see? Other cars, the road, buildings?

GET YOUR EYES BACK ON THE ROAD! (Sorry, I was worried about you.)

Everything you see that was created by man was once nothing more than a thought. Someone had to conceive of the couch you're sitting on before the plans were made, the materials were gathered, and the work was done to make it and ship it to the store where you purchased it. Someone had to dream up the house you're living in before it was built. I had to think of every word in this book in order to write it so you could read it right now.

Everything that gets done in this world begins as a thought. From the first automobile to manned spaceflight to the Internet to cancer treatments to magnificent symphonies and works of art, everything had its origins in a thought. I find that incredible.

The same holds true for who you are. Everything you do and everything you are begins as one of your thoughts.

A man is what he thinks about all day long.

–Ralph Waldo Emerson, American essayist, lecturer, and poet

You Think, Therefore You Do, Therefore You Are

You become what you think about *the most*. Or, you become what you think about all day long. You create what you think about all day long. You develop solutions and ideas for what you think about all day long.

What you think about leads you to who you are, who you will become, what you do, and what you will do.

That sounds fantastic and unbelievable, doesn't it? Test it to see if it makes sense to you. What have you ever done that didn't begin with a thought? When have you ever made changes in your life that didn't begin with a thought?

Ninety percent of our thoughts are automatic. We don't even realize we are thinking them. That's our biggest problem with making changes. We have to change our thoughts before we can change our behavior. If we keep thinking the same things we've thought every day, we will keep doing the same things. Is it any wonder we're not getting any closer to our goals?

So what are you thinking about all day long? Are they your original thoughts, or are they thoughts other people put in your head? Are they positive or negative thoughts? Are they helping or hurting you? Stop reading right now and take some time to think about and answer each of those questions. Write down the answers. It will help change your life.

Whatever you focus on, you will tend to get more of it. Your conscious and subconscious minds will get the message that this is important to you. They will work all day and all night to help you with whatever it is you are thinking about. Isn't that amazing?

> *All that we are is the result of what we have thought. The mind is everything. What we think we become.*
>
> –Gautama Siddhartha, the founder of Buddhism

Your subconscious mind doesn't care if you're thinking negative or positive thoughts. Since you're focusing on it you must want more of it, right? That's the way your brain works.

Earl Nightingale, in his seminal work *The Strangest Secret Ever Told*, relates it to how a farmer and his field work together. Whether he plants corn or poison ivy in his field, the field doesn't care. It will grow one just as well as the other. The field doesn't judge what you're planting. If the farmer plants corn and cares for it, the field will yield a wonderful crop of corn for him. If the farmer plants poison ivy, the field doesn't listen to the farmer say, "No, I don't want poison ivy, I want corn." All the field knows is the farmer planted poison ivy, so that is what he is going to get.

What are you planting in your mind every day?

Be *careful* what you think about. Are you thinking about solutions or problems? Important goals or busy work? Making things better or complaining?

If you constantly think negative thoughts, don't be surprised if you get negative outcomes. I'm sure you've seen this in your own life. When you get in a funk and start complaining about things you can quickly get in a downward spiral that is difficult to get out of.

Most of us have also experienced the opposite. We've had something good happen, we've focused on it, and then we've gotten on a roll. We feel like we're in the zone and everything is working out for us.

If you don't like the results you are getting in life, take a look at what you're thinking about. Remember, all action starts with a thought—conscious or unconscious. Most of us get into habits that we tend to follow every day like robots. We stop engaging our conscious mind and go about our days on autopilot.

What do you do the same every day - from when you wake up to how you get ready for work to how you drive to the office to how you tackle the day's tasks to how you eat dinner and what you do in your spare time? What are you telling yourself in your head all day as you keep repeating your habits? What are you thinking about all day long?

That is what you *are* and what you are *becoming.*

Change Your Thinking to Change Your Results

The world as we have created it is a process of our thinking. It cannot be changed without changing our thinking.

–Albert Einstein, theoretical physicist and philosopher of science

What do you think the chances are for your life to change if you keep thinking and doing the same things that got you to where you are now? If we want things to change we must break these thinking and doing habits and create new ones.

Earlier, you decided what you want. Now, the key is to think about what you want—to keep it in the forefront of your mind as often as possible.

It may sound difficult to keep thinking about what you want. You have a lot of things going on in your life. You are thinking about your job, your family, your relationships, and what you are doing at any moment in the day. All of that is true. But you are already thinking about much more than what you are actually doing all day long.

We all talk to ourselves all day long. We say things like:

"Why do I have to get up so early?"

"This meeting is so boring."

"I am never going to get that promotion."

"How did he get so successful? I guess I'm just not as lucky as he is."

"I'll never achieve my dreams."

Or we say things like:

"This is going to be a great day."

"Things keep working out for me."

Go!

"I am really on a roll."

"I'm finishing my sales presentation today."

"I can do this."

Pay attention to your internal talk for a couple of days. Actually write down what you're saying to yourself all day long. Set your smart phone timer to go off every 15 minutes. Write down exactly what you're thinking about when the timer sounds. When you catch yourself thinking positive or negative thoughts throughout the day, jot those down as well. At the end of the day, review your notes. What did you find out about your thoughts and your self-talk?

If you're like most people and don't actively work at controlling your thinking, you were probably shocked at just how negative your self-talk is.

When you practice and become proficient in controlling your thoughts you will be amazed at the difference it will make in every aspect of your life. It doesn't take long to turn around your thoughts, your attitude, your actions, and your results. Become intentional about what you think about all day long and watch the changes that follow.

Rational Emotive Therapy

> *Men are disturbed not by events, but by the views which they take of them.*
>
> –Epictetus, Greek Stoic philosopher, former slave

Psychologist Albert Ellis was the founder of something called Rational Emotive Therapy. He did a lot of work on how our thoughts determine our moods and behaviors. His contention was that it's not what happens to us that determines how we feel and act. It's how we *think about* what happens to us that determines how we feel and act. He saw it happening in an A-B-C pattern.

A – An Activating event in your life that triggers negative or positive thoughts. It could be something small like stepping in a mud puddle in your brand-new shoes or something big like the death of a parent.

B – The Beliefs or thoughts you think about the event.

C – The Consequences, feelings, and behaviors that come from your beliefs and thoughts.

It is not the activating event that determines your feelings and behaviors, it is your beliefs and thoughts about the activating event. Two people can experience very similar events but respond with totally different feelings and behaviors. The difference wasn't the event, it was the way each of them chose to think about the event.

Imagine missing the bus on your way to work. You could think, "This stuff always happens to me. Now my day is ruined and I might even get fired. Nothing ever works out for me." Or, you could think, "I missed the bus. Oh well, I'll sit on the bench and get some work done while I'm waiting for the next one. I was rushing around too much this morning anyway. Maybe I'll make a new friend on the next bus. Who knows what good things might happen from this." Very different feelings and behaviors will result from the different thoughts you had from the exact same event.

Ellis pointed out that we often have irrational thoughts that lead us to negative feelings and beliefs. If a boyfriend or girlfriend breaks up with us we might think, "I'm unlovable. No one will ever want to marry me." If we get fired we might think, "This is the worst thing that could ever happen to me. I'm going to lose my job and end up on welfare." Or maybe you believe that you can never be happy because of things that have happened in your past. The more you tell yourself these things the truer they become for you.

However, if you can catch yourself thinking these irrational thoughts, stop them and change them to more positive thoughts, then those new thoughts become true for you. Replace the thinking in the above scenarios with new thinking.

"It's good we broke up now. We weren't a good match. Now I'm free to find my future husband." "I wasn't planning on getting fired. There will be some things I have to work out. But I knew this wasn't really the job for me. I'm going to focus on getting a job I'm passionate about and can excel at. This could actually be a good thing for me. Maybe I'll even use this time to start my own business. I have savings that can keep me going until I find my new source of income. I'm going to be fine."

"I've had some challenges in my past, but those challenges don't determine who I am, what I will do, or who I will become in the future. I am going to learn and grow from my past and create the future I want."

Let's go a bit deeper on this: Most of us think irrational thoughts and ask ourselves irrational questions every day. When something goes wrong in your life do you ask negative questions like, "Why does this always happen to me?" or, "Why do I always fail?" or my personal favorite, "How could I be so stupid?"

These questions won't help you. They're irrational and based on false premises. Honestly, does "this" *always* happen to you? Do you *always* fail? Are you truly stupid, or did you just do something you wish you wouldn't have? Do only bad things happen to you *every* day? Of course not. If we focus on the negative, it can begin to seem that way to us. But when we examine our lives closely, we know this is nonsense.

When you notice you're asking those types of negative, false questions, stop it. Yell, "Stop!" out loud or in your head. Scratch those records you keep playing in your head so you can't hear them anymore.

Start asking positive questions like, "How can I use this challenge for my good?" or "What can I learn from this experience and act on right now?" "How can I improve my outcome next time?"

Suppose you got a flat tire on your way to work. You immediately start thinking, "Why does this always happen to me? Why is my luck so bad? What did I do to deserve this? I'm going to be late to work, the boss is going to think I'm irresponsible and I'm going to get fired. Then I won't have the money to pay my mortgage and I'm going to lose my house. This is the worst day of my life!"

Once you start telling yourself these awful things you need to notice it and stop them. Fight back! Have a conversation with yourself in your head and say, “This doesn’t always happen to me. I haven’t had a flat tire in two years. I can’t remember the last time I checked my tires. I better check the other three and see if it’s time to get some new ones so this doesn’t happen to me again. I don’t have bad luck, and I didn’t do anything to deserve this, I just didn’t keep up with the condition of my tires. This happens to everyone from time to time. I will text my boss right now to let him know what’s happened and that I’ll be in as soon as I can. She knows what a responsible employee I am and she will understand. This is not going to cost me my job, and I’m certainly not going to lose my house over this.”

After you handle the situation, keep your conversation with yourself going. “What can I learn from this? Well, I can pay more attention to my car and make sure to maintain it better, and I can buy roadside assistance just in case this ever happens again.”

Try this out in your life and see what happens. Practice changing how you view activating events in your life. Reframe them in the best way possible. Think positively about the best way to handle every situation that comes your way.

This doesn’t mean you will never feel sad or angry or upset. It just means you will not overreact and put yourself into such a negative place that you can’t make rational decisions to move forward with your goals.

Spend Some Time Every Day Just Thinking

> *Thinking is the hardest work there is, which is probably the reason so few engage in it.*
>
> –Henry Ford

Really thinking about something, engaging your whole brain—your entire being—into thinking about something is very hard work. But it is unbelievably rewarding.

When you spend purposeful, planned time thinking every day you will see your ideas, creativity, and success grow exponentially.

Legend has it that when Einstein was working as a professor he would spend some time every day with his feet up on his desk, seemingly doing nothing. One day the president of the university came in and ordered him to get to work. Einstein replied, "I am making gold bricks in my head."

He was thinking, imagining, creating, and visualizing great ideas that would be worth their weight in gold. He wasn't being lazy. He was making gold bricks in his head.

Greg, I'm busy. I barely have time to breathe. When would I have time to turn everything off, put my feet up, and just think?

There is ample time to think throughout the day no matter how busy we get. Stimulate your conscious and unconscious minds to focus on what you want by reading your goals every morning, noon, and night. Let your mind dwell on them when you're doing repetitive, low-thought tasks like driving to work with the radio off, walking, running, gardening, cleaning the house, showering, etc.

When thoughts come to you, write them down right away. If you're driving, use your smart phone to record them. (Please keep your eyes on the road and use the voice commands.)

You can also set aside 15 minutes a day to meditate and pray and then let your mind focus on what you want.

You will be amazed at the ideas that "come out of nowhere" while you're shampooing your hair, or making it up that final climb on your jog, or when you're 20 minutes into your evening commute.

When you do these things consistently, you get bonus thinking that takes no effort on your part. Your subconscious will go into high gear for you while you sleep. It's happened to you before, hasn't it? Something's been weighing on your mind and you've thought about it all day. You still didn't resolve it and you ended up going to bed. Miraculously, you awoke in the morning with the solution to your problem or a new way of looking at it.

The human mind is an amazing thing. Why not learn how to use it and point it in the right direction to help you get what you want?

Techniques from the Masters

- You become what you think about.
- Remember everything made by man and done by man began as a thought.
- Most of your thoughts are automatic. Reprogram your thoughts so you are automatically thinking more about what you want.
- Spend planned, purposeful time thinking about what you want every day. You will be surprised by the ideas and creativity that begin to come to you.
- Read your goals every day when you wake up, at lunch, and right before bed. Let your mind dwell on them when you're doing repetitive, low-skill tasks.
- Set aside 15 minutes a day to pray and meditate on what you want.
- Practice changing how you view activating events in your life. Reframe them in the best way possible. Think positively about the best way to handle every situation that comes your way.

You Are Talented and "Lucky" Enough

Everything You Need to Pursue Your
Passionate Purpose You Already Have or You Can Learn

I busted a mirror and got seven years bad luck, but my lawyer thinks he can get me five.

–Stephen Wright, comedian, actor, author

Sure, Greg, all this sounds great, but we all know that your success really comes down to how lucky you are and how much talent you were born with.

For just a second forget about whether that's true or not. Let me ask you a question. If you really believe that your success is out of your control and is determined by luck and talent, will that belief help you achieve your goals?

A recent CNN poll asked 1,003 adult Americans:

"Do you agree or disagree: The American dream has become impossible for most people to achieve."

Sadly, 59 percent agreed. Some 63 percent of those aged 18-34 agreed that the American dream is virtually dead.

What do you think?

If you believe the American dream is dead, you're right.

If you believe you will never be a success, you're right.

If you believe you're not lucky enough, or not talented enough, you're right … for you.

How would you ever expect to succeed with those beliefs holding you back? Unfortunately, we are bombarded daily by so-called leaders, experts, and friends telling us how we will never be able to fulfill our dreams and accomplish our goals. Some of them are trying to "help." Some of them are jealous. Some of them are trying to excuse themselves for not reaching the level of success they'd once hoped for.

Regardless of their reasons for feeding us that defeatist philosophy, if we believe them, they will be right. But if we reject those negative beliefs and stay focused on our Passionate Purpose we will achieve more than we ever thought we could.

If you believe you can find the husband or wife of your dreams, you're right.

If you believe you can run a marathon, you're right.

If you believe you can become a financial success, you're right.

If the American dream really is dead, then how are people still going from rags to riches every day in this country? How are some people able to go from nothing to super successful in one generation? Luck?

I Don't Believe in Luck

> *Good luck is a lazy man's estimate of a worker's success.*
>
> –Anonymous

I believe in preparing yourself to take advantage of opportunities that will appear as you stay focused on your goals. If you are constantly thinking about where you want to go and improving yourself in every way to be the person you need to be to achieve the success you are working towards, you will see opportunities appear with increasing frequency. Is that luck? No. It's the result of hard work and taking consistent action.

You Are Talented and "Lucky" Enough

A friend of mine was telling me about a guy he knows who got "really lucky." He said the guy went from being a radio producer in a midsize market to becoming a program director in the second biggest market in America in just two years. "What a lucky guy." My friend seemed bummed about this because he didn't think he had that kind of luck and didn't think he would be able to attain the same success his friend had.

I asked exactly what the other guy did on his way to becoming so "lucky." Well, it turns out that he had put in a lot of time and hard work to become an excellent producer in that midsize market. Then he moved out to San Francisco and went to every station in town to let them know who he was and what he could do to help them as an accomplished radio producer. He left them demos of his work. He had an excellent reputation in the field and impeccable references that he had developed through his years of professional work.

When one of the stations had an opening, was it "lucky" that they hired him? I think it was hard work and preparation and lots of activity meeting up with an opportunity. How many people would have liked that job but never went to the station to tell them who they were? How many didn't put in the hard work to become one of the best in their field? How many gave up because they weren't "lucky" enough?

At the new job, he put in long hours as a producer and started working as an assistant program director as well. His work at the station in San Francisco increased his reputation in the radio world. All this gave him the experience he needed to be ready when an opportunity came open for a program director (a big step up from producer) in the second-biggest market in America.

None of this was luck. All of these opportunities would have meant nothing to this guy if he hadn't worked hard, prepared himself, and been ready to step up when given the chance.

There are opportunities like this all the time for every goal you have. Whether or not you will be ready to seize them will have nothing to do with "luck."

Some people would rather believe that it all comes down to luck. For them, believing in luck is a way to feel better about themselves when they don't reach their goals or someone else is achieving the success they want.

I believe in luck: how else can you explain the success of those you dislike?

–Jean Cocteau, French writer, designer, playwright, artist, and filmmaker

The question remains. Does your belief in "luck" help or hurt you?

Nationally Syndicated Because of Luck?

I find that the harder I work, the more luck I seem to have.

–Thomas Jefferson

Before and after I had my own syndicated radio talk show, I guest hosted for other national programs. I can't tell you how many people would comment on how "lucky" I was to fill in for so many big-name radio stars.

The truth is luck had nothing to do with it. I worked hard at becoming a good host. I asked for, and acted on, the constructive criticism that I received and kept getting better. I kept making demo tapes and sending them to program directors all across the country.

Then I started asking the producers and hosts of the national shows if I could fill in for them when they were on vacation or whenever they needed someone on short notice.

Now, when one of these hosts got sick and they needed someone to fill in at the last second, was it "luck" that I often got the call? Once I filled in and they liked what they heard, was it "luck" that I was asked to guest host again?

When a smaller syndication company was looking for a new national host, was it "luck" that I was one of the ones they interviewed for the position?

I like what Don Sutton says: "Luck is the by-product of busting your fanny."

> *Shallow people believe in luck and in circumstances; Strong people believe in cause and effect.*
>
> –Ralph Waldo Emerson

You Can Create Your Own "Luck"

Although I don't believe in what most people mean when they use the word "luck," I do believe that you can create and act upon great opportunities that come your way when you constantly look for them.

Richard Wiseman is Professor of the Public Understanding of Psychology at the University of Hertfordshire in the United Kingdom. He has done some interesting work on this. Wiseman has studied hundreds of self-described lucky and unlucky people. He found that rather than being born with or without it, people really do make their own luck.

Chance, fate, destiny, whatever you want to call it, doesn't determine your success or failure. Instead, your thoughts and behavior largely determine how "lucky" you will be.

Professor Wiseman discovered four common principles among his subjects on becoming "lucky."

1) Maximize Chance Opportunities: LPs (lucky people) are open to what some people call chance opportunities or coincidences or serendipity. They look for them and act upon them. They're also open to new ideas and experiences.

2) Listen to Lucky Hunches: LPs pay attention to that little voice inside them. They go with their gut.

3) Expect Good Fortune: LPs have a strong belief that things are going to work out for them. They always expect the best. This helps them create the future they want. LPs keep going in bad times because of their belief that good things are coming. It also helps them relate well with others. This helps them network and creates even more opportunities for them.

4) Turn Bad Luck to Good: Finally, when bad things happen to LPs they don't think about them the same way unlucky people do. Instead, they truly look on the bright side. "It's not that bad." "It could have been worse." "I can learn something from this." "Here's how I can fix it."

This allows LPs to quickly get back in the good-luck groove.

To learn more about how to increase your good "luck" check out Professor Wiseman's book, *The Luck Factor.* Then put some of these ideas into practice and let me know how "lucky" you become.

Go!

> *Luck? I don't know anything about luck. I've never banked on it, and I'm afraid of people who do. Luck to me is something else: hard work—and realizing what is opportunity and what isn't.*
>
> –Lucille Ball, comedienne, actor

You Are Talented Enough

OK, maybe you create your own luck, but you can't deny that some people are just more talented than others. You're born with talent. There's nothing I can do about that.

The bad news is: If you believe that, you are going to have a much harder time reaching your goals.

The good news is the latest research shows this idea of "talent" just isn't true. I recommend two books on this for more information: *Talent Is Overrated,* by Geoff Colvin and *The Talent Code*, by Daniel Coyle.

Both books found the data show no proof of what most of us call talent. Even people who seem to show an uncanny ability at a young age at playing an instrument or a sport really aren't more "talented" than other children. The researchers found they have simply practiced more, practiced better, and often been instructed better, than the other children. In fact, the biggest indicator of "precocious ability" in children was how long they practiced every week.

That is very encouraging. That means we can do it too. You've probably heard of the 10,000-hour rule popularized by Malcolm Gladwell in his book *Outliers.* The rule says it takes around 10,000 hours of practice to become an expert or world-class in your field. The talent books found essentially the same thing.

Don't forget that the *kind* of practice you do matters as much as the amount of time you practice. Deep, deliberative practice is what you are looking for. Colvin describes deliberate practice this way:

> *"Deliberate practice is characterized by several elements, each worth examining. It is activity designed specifically to improve performance, often with a teacher's help; it can be repeated a lot; feedback on results is continuously available; it's highly demanding mentally, whether the activity is purely intellectual such as chess or business-related activities, or heavily physical, such as sports; and it isn't much fun."* [1]

Coyle sees it only slightly differently and calls it deep practice. He says you are looking to stay in the "sweet spot" of struggle for as long as you can. Catching and correcting your errors. It's very mentally taxing and most cannot do it for long periods. However, if you can stay in deep practice, you can do in ten minutes what it would take weeks of regular practice to do.

> *"The sweet spot: that productive, uncomfortable terrain located just beyond our current abilities, where our reach exceeds our grasp. Deep practice is not simply about struggling; it's about seeking a particular struggle, which involves a cycle of distinct actions."* [2]

Coyle found that breaking skills into chunks, slowing down the skill you're practicing and doing a little every day were keys. All-nighters don't make up for a week of no practice. But more important than the time put in was the time spent in deep practice.

Slowing it down so you can play the musical phrase or do the skill correctly is what matters. Coyle quotes a famous football coach who says, "It's not how fast you can do it. It's how slow you can do it correctly."

I've tried this with my guitar practice with great results. This is the way world-class athletes have always worked on their skills.

Sure, Greg, but I'm not trying to become an expert musician or professional athlete. I'm at the stage of my life where I'm working on my career.

Understood. Here's the thing. Deep practice is something we rarely do for our careers. We simply go to work every day and just expect to become great by doing the same thing over and over. But what if you started doing some deep practice for your career?

If you're in sales, you should be breaking down your sales presentations into chunks and practicing them until you're super smooth. Ask a colleague you trust to watch your presentation and give you immediate feedback. Tweak it and make it even better. What would happen to your career if you became world-class at making sales presentations?

If you're a surgeon you can do deep practice on medical dummies and cadavers to work on the intricate skills you will need to do your next difficult surgery. In fact, that's what new doctors do. Why don't we do that equivalent in whatever career we have?

You Are Talented and "Lucky" Enough

When I started out in radio as a producer my desire was to be on air. I had no training or education in how to do a talk radio show. I spent a lot of time listening to all types of talk radio. Then I started pretending to have my own show. I would sneak into the studios after hours and record my best. On the way home I would listen to the tape in the car and see what I liked and what I could do to improve.

People I trusted in radio were kind enough to listen to my tapes and give me constructive criticism. By the time I finally went on the air with my own show, I had done countless hours of my "fake" show.

What can you do in your career to deep practice the skills you need to become world-class?

Techniques from the Masters

- Practice being deliberate in your thinking. Positive thinking won't magically make something happen for you, but it will lead you in the right direction and encourage you. Negative thinking will bring you down and make it very difficult to reach your goals.
- Remember that you make your own "luck." Your thoughts and behavior are much more important in helping you make the most of the opportunities coming your way than fate or chance.
- Study and practice the four main ways to become more "lucky."
- Develop deep practice strategies for every skill you are trying to improve. Most people stop practicing things when they become adults. Almost no one "deep practices" their job. If you do, you will have an enormous advantage.
- Read the books *The Talent Code, Talent Is Overrated,* and *The Luck Factor*.
- Good luck!

Mindset

Back to Work on Your New Mindset

In order for you to change your life and pursue your Passionate Purpose as far as it will take you, you need the proper mindset. Extensive research shows that most successful people have a mindset that is positive and optimistic. They believe they have control over their lives, not that events control them. They believe that being successful helps everyone and exploits no one. Most successful people have a mindset focused on growth and learning what they need to achieve all their goals. They have a mindset that asks, "Why not?" "What can I learn from this?" "What if?" They have confidence in their abilities to do what is necessary to win.

Most successful people don't believe they are in competition with everyone they meet. They understand they are creating the extraordinary life they want. They don't have to take from someone else to do that. They don't believe everyone is out to get them.

I have declared myself a Dionarap. I believe that everyone is out to *help* me. (OK, yes, it's just paranoid spelled backwards. You got me.)

A Positive Mindset

> *The greatest discovery of my generation is that human beings can alter their lives by altering their attitudes of mind.*
>
> –William James, American philosopher and psychologist

Did you hear about the optimist and the pessimist living next door to each other? They both had to get up at 6:00 a.m. to get to work on time at similar jobs. The optimist jumped up when he heard the "opportunity clock" go off. (Thank you, Zig Ziglar.) He pulled the blinds open and yelled, "Good morning, God!" The pessimist hit the snooze on his alarm clock five times before he finally dragged himself out of bed. He peeked through his blinds and growled, "Good god, it's morning."

Who do you think is going to have a better day?

Get ready for an amazing insight coming at you. People with a good, positive, optimistic attitude tend to enjoy their day more and accomplish more than people with a negative, depressing, pessimistic attitude. See, I told you—deep insight. You're welcome.

We know this from research and from our own experience. But how do we create and maintain the positive mindset we need to reach all our goals?

One way is to start every morning by thinking about all the great things in your life. An attitude of gratitude is a phenomenal way to begin the day. For most of us it's pretty easy coming up with a list of all the great things in our lives. Take some time right now. For the next five minutes write down every single thing you are grateful for. Make your list now. Go!

Was this challenging for you? I know some people who are so depressed that it's hard for them to even start a list like that. But no matter where you are in your life right now, I know there are things you can find to be grateful and thankful for. Hey, you're breathing and you can read. There are two things to get you started. That may sound silly, but you'd be surprised how just starting your grateful list with something as simple as that can get you on the right track.

I have a routine I go through every day when I wake up that gets me up on the right side of the bed. I'm a Christian, so for me this ties into my religion. But you can use the same type of technique whether you're religious or not. Instead of a thankful prayer list, simply make it your gratitude list.

As I slowly enter the land of the living, I start to pray. I start thanking God for all my blessings. I thank him for my wife, my children, my extended family, and my friends. I thank him for the fact that I have more than enough to provide my family with food, clothing, and shelter. I praise God for the fact that I was born in the United States of America and I have so many opportunities to create a life of abundance for myself and enough to help others as well. I give thanks for having jobs that I love, and I'm grateful for my excellent health.

As I'm saying my prayers, I'm creating beautiful images in my head of everything I'm praying about. As I do this, I can feel my body and spirit coming more and more alive. Feelings of peace and happiness and ambition well up within me and I begin to feel excited about getting out of bed and starting the day. I spend about thee minutes doing this. (I know this sounds kind of touchy-feely, but if you try it for a few days I think you will be amazed at the results you get.)

After I'm done giving thanks, I spend the next three to five minutes being grateful for my future life with all my major goals achieved. Even though it's about my future life, I put everything in the present tense as if I'm already living the life I want. We are getting our conscious and subconscious minds focused on our goals, and the best way to do that is to put everything we want in the present tense.

I visualize pursuing my Passionate Purpose at the ultimate level. I imagine achieving my goals in every aspect of my life. If you really want to get excited about your future, describe it in great detail and imagine how it will look, feel, sound, smell, and taste. Get your emotions into it. Play the movie of your extraordinary life in your head. It's better than any blockbuster at the multiplex.

One of the things on my future gratitude list is my dream home right on the beach. I'm a huge fan of the ocean and have spent much of my life surfing, swimming, sunbathing, and walking on the sand. I have written down a detailed description of what this home will look like and what it will be like to live the rest of my life there. When I imagine waking up in my dream home and drinking my morning tea on my back deck while watching the waves roll in, I almost feel like I'm living there right now.

The more real you make this, the more excited you will become to take on the day, and the more your subconscious mind will help you pursue your goals. I am amazed how happy this exercise makes me every day.

I've never been a "morning person," but I've found that if you work at it, you can become one. I like to wake up to nature sounds instead of a buzzer alarm. It's a very pleasant way for me to gradually rise up out of the depths of sleep.

There are some great apps for your smartphone now that have pleasant sounds to start your day with. Some of them even track your sleep patterns and wake you when it's easiest on your body. Simply search for them on your Apple Store or Google Play app.

Greg, I can't get up to nature sounds. I need a loud, blaring alarm. And I can't take five to ten minutes to wake up. I have to jump out of bed so I can get to work on time.

Hey, I get it. You're busy and a deep sleeper. But I am confident if you go to bed 15 minutes earlier than you do right now, set your alarm 15 minutes earlier than normal, and go through this new wakeup routine for two weeks, you will enjoy it so much that it will become your new morning ritual. Try it. What have you got to lose?

Growth and Fixed Mindsets

Carol Dweck's book, *Mindset: The New Psychology of Success*, suggests there are two types of mindsets. A *fixed mindset* believes that your intelligence, talents, skills, and personality are largely set and there is little you can do to change them. A *growth mindset* believes that you can learn, grow, and improve anything through effort, experience, and practice. There may be upper limits we can reach based on what we were born with, but nothing is set in stone.

Guess which mindset Professor Dweck's research showed was seen more in successful people? It's so obvious, I'm surprised we even needed to study it.

Mindset explains that people with a fixed mindset play it safe to protect their positive beliefs about themselves. If you're smart, things come easy to you. So if something is hard, it's better not to do it. Otherwise, you will have to conclude you're not smart. Dweck found that when these people didn't do well at something, it threatened their belief in their fixed intelligence so much that some of them would lie about their performance to protect themselves.

Have you ever had a boss who took all the credit but none of the blame? If he received constructive criticism, he would blame the messenger? When you brought a new idea, he would reject it immediately and even become angry with you for trying to move the company to keep up with the times? Those are some of the traits of a fixed mindset manager.

People with the growth mindset are more willing to try new things and struggle with hard tasks. They get excited about learning and getting better. They're willing to take more risks because every little failure they might endure isn't proof that they're not smart. It's just a bump in the road as they learn and grow. Growth mindset people actually *enjoy* that process.

This type of boss welcomes new ideas and sees them as opportunities for everyone on the team, including him, to stretch, learn, and grow. He can take criticism in stride knowing that we all have weak spots and with hard work we can develop new skills and get better where we need to. He can share credit with his employees because he doesn't have to prove he's the smartest person in the room.

Which type of manager do you want to be or work for?

Your mindset appears to form at a very young age. Dweck gives an example of the differences in the fixed and growth mindsets in an experiment they did with four-year-olds.

> *"We offered four-year-olds a choice: They could redo an easy jigsaw puzzle or they could try a harder one. Even at this tender age, children with the fixed mindset—the ones who believed in fixed traits—stuck with the safe one. Kids who are born smart 'don't make mistakes,' they told us."* [1]

The children with the growth mindsets gravitated to the harder puzzles. They were energized by the challenge and how the more difficult puzzles led to them increasing their skills. One kid even asked if he could take some of the harder puzzles home.

The growth mindset leads you to try new things, take on new challenges, learn from criticism, share credit with your team, and keep pace with changes in your field.

The fixed mindset leads you to play it safe, react angrily to criticism, blame others and circumstances for your failures, and avoid new challenges and new ideas for fear of having your intelligence and abilities questioned or threatened.

Well, that's just great, Greg. Reading this, I have figured out that I'm a fixed mindset person. So I guess I'm not going to succeed.

Whoa, tap the brakes, Speed Racer. That type of thinking *is* the fixed mindset thinking. You're born one way and that's it. Well, I have good news for you. Almost no one has a totally fixed mindset; we are all somewhere on the continuum between fixed and growth. Here's some more good news: You can *choose* your mindset. It's not set in stone.

When you are about to try something new, get yourself into the growth mindset before you begin. Tell yourself you are about to learn and grow. You might not get it right immediately, but if you put in the effort you will succeed. When you make a mistake, tell yourself you just learned something and you're now one step closer to reaching your goal.

Then pay attention to your self-talk; you can catch yourself making limiting, fixed mindset statements and stop them in their tracks. Imagine you have an opportunity to lead a new project at work. There are some new concepts involved in it and you're not sure about it. Your fixed mindset thoughts might say, "This is risky. What if I fail? I'll be a failure. Maybe I'm just not smart enough or talented enough to do this."

When you notice these thoughts, yell "Stop!" inside your head. Replace those thoughts with growth mindset thoughts. Say to yourself, "This is a great opportunity for me. I may not know everything about this right now, but with hard work I can learn what I need. This will be a great chance to grow and expand my skills. Let's go for it."

I highly recommend Dweck's *Mindset: The New Psychology of Success* for more details on the different mindsets and how to become a growth mindset person.

A Successful Mindset

> *A pessimist sees the difficulty in every opportunity; an optimist sees the opportunity in every difficulty.*
>
> –Winston S. Churchill, former prime minister of the United Kingdom

People pursuing their Passionate Purpose wake up optimistic. They look forward to what they're going to get out of each day. They see opportunities everywhere. They are spending most of their time thinking about what they want to do and accomplish. They are expecting to work hard and enjoy the work. They know that if they keep to their goals and plans they will eventually live the life that others only dream of. If they stay focused, every kind of success will follow.

This can become very difficult if you have a mindset of scarcity and believe if you earn more others will get less. Maybe you think it's greedy to want success, or you believe you have to cheat and exploit others to achieve. That's going to stop your progress in its tracks. Who wants to be a jerk and step on people to get ahead? If that's how you believe it works, you will continue to sabotage your own success in order to avoid turning into that awful person you always swore you wouldn't become.

So what are your thoughts about success? How about earning more money?

Too Much Success?

One of the biggest obstacles to success for some people is what they were taught as children. Quite often society, our parents, and our schools teach us to limit our dreams or, worse yet, that too much success can be bad.

OK, right now you're thinking to yourself, "Greg has gone cuckoo for Cocoa Puffs again. No one says that too much success is a bad thing." Au contraire mon frère. You hear it all the time. Look at what's being said about CEOs and corporations. Things like, "That guy makes too much money," or, "That company makes obscene profits," or, "No one is worth that salary." All of those statements are saying that too much success is bad.

We have a weird situation in America where we like to see the little guy go from rags to riches, as long as the riches don't get too great. Once he hits a certain level, he suddenly becomes someone who's exploiting the people.

Of course, there are people who step on others, act unethically, or even illegally to get ahead. Most of the time, they eventually have things collapse around them. Their businesses go under, they get divorced, maybe they even go to jail and their life becomes miserable. My dad has a saying about people who behave that way, "Time wounds all heels."

But most people who succeed do it the right way. They end up getting what they want by providing other people with what they need and want. They run their affairs with the Golden Rule as their guide.

Money Is *Not* the Root of All Evil, and the Bible Doesn't Say It Is

Much of society teaches that money is bad or evil. The people who make a lot of money are uncaring and coldhearted, we are told. Some people use the Bible to justify this. They claim it says money is the root of all evil. But that's not what it really says.

> *For the* **love** *of money is a root of all kinds of evil. Some people, eager for money, have wandered from the faith and pierced themselves with many griefs.*
>
> –1 Timothy 6:10, NIV (emphasis added)

The Bible is clearly saying that the ***love*** of money is the root of all evil. When you love money more than you love God, more than you love your family, more than you love what is right, that's when you're going down the wrong path. You're turning money into your idol, your god. But money itself is neutral. The *pursuit* of money and the *use* of money can be good or evil.

When the leadership of Enron cooked the books to make it look like they had a better financial statement than they did, their love of money was evil. When politicians take bribes or unethical campaign contributions, their love of money is evil. When lending officers gave subprime loans to people they knew could not afford them and borrowers took loans they knew they could not pay back, their love of money was evil. When a mechanic makes unnecessary repairs on a car just to get a little more cash, his love of money is evil.

But money can be used to do wondrous good works. It can lead to starting or growing a business that provides jobs and income for countless families. Money can equal charity, medicine, food, clothing, shelter, schools, books, and much more. Money can help get you everything you need to physically survive and to help others. It can provide you time to do what you love. Money makes everything you want to do, have, and be easier.

Profits made by companies big and small can be used to expand the business and create new jobs, to give their current employees raises and stock options, and to donate to worthy charities in the community.

With all the bad press that CEOs and businessmen have been receiving lately, I want to praise one.

He's a man who has shown great loyalty to his employees, operators, and customers. He worked one full year without a salary because times were hard and he didn't want his operators to take a bigger hit if he could help it. He's now worth over $1.3 billion and gives millions to charity every year. And it all started from growing up poor during the Great Depression.

Sam was an entrepreneur from an early age. He was constantly working on ways to help the family earn enough to get by. By the time he was 8 years old, Sam was selling soda. He would buy six-packs at the local store and then peddle them door to door.

He moved on from soda to magazines and then got a paper route. This was great training for his future life as a businessman. Sam was responsible for finding new customers and keeping his old ones happy. He had to buy and sell the papers. It taught him how you have to buy wholesale and sell retail at a price that will make you a profit, but not drive customers away.

Sam decided to open a restaurant with his brother. It wasn't easy and they worked hard to do anything and everything the business needed. They even did the construction to finish off their new place.

It was small, with only four tables and 10 seats at the counter. But it made money almost right away. Then, tragedy struck. Sam's brother died in a plane crash. The new restaurant Sam started burned down. He was down, but still had an idea burning in him.

His mom had a way of cooking that made the meat juicy and delicious. Sam knew if he could use her method to make sandwiches, people would love them. Going back to the skills he learned on his paper route, he made a deal with an airline. They had scraps of meat left when they cut it up to make their dinners. They were willing to sell the small pieces to Sam for a great price. They were the perfect size for his sandwiches. His customers loved them and he knew he had something.

Sam opened his first fast food restaurant in 1967. He used the income from his original restaurant to slowly build new ones. Sam worked hard, but wasn't able to really start making money for himself until his 17th restaurant opened.

The late '70s and early '80s were particularly difficult. In 1982, with his operators and employees having a tough time making ends meet, Sam opted to go without a salary.

You have probably had Sam's famous sandwich, and you have probably seen the cows that promote it. (Sam) S. Truett Cathy was the founder of Chick-fil-A restaurants and the inventor of the fast food chicken sandwich.

At the time of his passing, he had more than 1,200 stores and tens of thousands of happy employees. He lived his Christian-based business principles through every store he opened. He kept every store closed on Sunday so he and his employees could have a day of rest and time to go to church. If it wasn't for that decision, S. Truett might have become another operator of Kentucky Fried Chicken.

A positive attitude is stressed with all employees, and it shows in the way they interact with the customers.

S. Truett gave away over $20 million in scholarships to his employees and millions more through his WinShape Center Foundation. He also created 14 long-term foster homes through his WinShape Homes program. Every year, Camp WinShape helps build the self-esteem of 1,700 young people.

No doubt S. Truett Cathy made a lot of money. There is also no doubt that he earned it and he has helped countless people with it. It doesn't seem like money is the root of all evil in this story, does it?

> *Nearly every moment of every day we have the opportunity to give something to someone else—our time, our love, our resources. I have always found more joy in giving when I did not expect anything in return.*
>
> –S. Truett Cathy

We Make Pies

"Well we're movin' on up,
To the east side.
To a deluxe apartment in the sky.
Movin' on up
To the east side.
We finally got a piece of the pie."

–Theme from the television show *The Jeffersons*

We live in a country with unparalleled opportunities to achieve financial independence. There is unlimited wealth to be created. And yet most Americans believe there is a finite amount of money available. If "the rich" take more it leaves less for everyone else.

This "if you get more pie I get less pie" myth has done enormous damage to our economic success as a country and discouraged countless Americans from achieving their financial dreams. Maybe people just watched too much of *The Jeffersons*.

George Jefferson didn't get a piece of the pie. He created wealth for himself and others. He provided a service (dry cleaning) people needed for a good price. As his business expanded, he provided more jobs for his employees. He paid more rent to more landlords in the areas he placed his dry cleaning stores. He helped his vendors by purchasing more equipment and materials to run his business. He invested his money and that money was used to start new businesses and expand old ones. It was used to hire even more employees and create even more wealth for all. He didn't make other people poorer because his dry cleaning stores succeeded. He made people richer. He *made* pies.

There is more than enough for everyone. It's like that old Doritos commercial: "Eat all you want, we'll make more!" We shouldn't worry about the size of our "piece of the pie," we should just keep making more pie. Even better, get this through your head: There is no pie. There are unlimited possibilities for all of us.

Think about this logically for a second. If there is some limited pie, how does our economy keep growing? How does the median income for Americans, adjusted for inflation, keep going up? Yes, we do have recessions in the business cycle, but overall our economy keeps growing. Most people in America who have a full-time job or who own a business see their incomes more than double in their lifetimes.

Think back to the first job you had. What was your salary? What is your yearly income now? I bet it has more than doubled, right? You can double it again with the right plan—and help people at the same time. Didn't George Jefferson help a lot more people every time he opened a new store? (Um, Greg, hold up, George Jefferson is a fictional TV character. I know, just go with it.) The best way to help people is to become as successful as you can at serving others with your Passionate Purpose.

You can become a millionaire without taking anything away from anyone else. In fact, as you become a millionaire you will be adding to the wealth in America. You will be creating, investing, saving, producing, and spending. You will be creating new jobs. Everybody wins.

Think back to all the jobs you have had. Have you ever worked for someone poorer than you? I haven't. I am thankful that richer people created those jobs for me and helped me provide for my family.

Good and Bad Competition

As long as we believe there is some finite amount of money out there, some "pie," we are going to remain at each other's throats scurrying around for crumbs while complaining that "the rich" are stealing the choicest pieces. That belief in scarcity and greed is going to make it much more difficult to achieve your goals.

When you believe there is a pie, everyone becomes your competition. Everyone becomes your enemy. What they gain, you lose. Their successes are your failures. You become paranoid and think that everyone is trying to take some of your pie. You won't want to work with someone or share an idea because you might have to give up some of your pie. It's truly a miserable existence. It leads to a great deal of envy, jealousy, anger, and frustration.

None of this helps you succeed. In fact, it breeds and grows the idea that your current and future financial standing is not up to you. It is determined by outside factors far beyond your control—things like who your parents are, where you went to school, and who you know. You believe the myth that only the rich get richer. Of course, the more you believe this, the more it is true—for you.

Become a Benevolent Millionaire

> *You can get everything in life you want if you will just help enough other people get what they want.*
>
> –Zig Ziglar, author and motivational speaker

I'm talking about becoming wealthy the right way, by helping people like S. Truett Cathy did and like George Jefferson did. (It's a TV show! He wasn't real! Stop with the George Jefferson analogy already! … Sorry.)

You can become a benevolent millionaire. You can help lift others as your success grows. The first thing to remember is what Zig Ziglar said. Your success will come from helping other people get what they want. That is a great service to your community. While you're doing that, why not do it the best way you can?

If you are starting your own company, you can treat your employees well with how you relate with them, what you pay them, and the benefits you provide for them. No matter what you do to earn your income you can become generous with how you spend and invest your money. You can choose to give to charities that you believe in.

You can become a mentor for someone and pass on all that you have learned. Invest in the next generation and you will be amazed how good it feels and how much you get out of it.

Imagine what would happen if everyone striving to multiply their income became a benevolent millionaire.

More Money = More for Everyone

Who helps more people, one social worker or Bill Gates? I'm sure the social worker is doing her best and is helping the people she comes into contact with, but she can't compete with the hundreds of millions of people Bill Gates has helped. Gates' company has made billions of dollars for himself, his investors, and his employees. He has created tens of thousands of jobs and helped increase the productivity of virtually every worker who uses a computer. He has donated billions of dollars to private charities and his company has paid billions of dollars in taxes—the type of taxes necessary for the salaries of social workers—every year. Gates has pledged to give his fortune away instead of passing it on to his children. Yet there are people who say he is too successful, too rich, spent too much money on a ridiculous house, and doesn't give enough of his money away. Wow.

I used to believe that people who made a lot of money weren't as nice or compassionate as I was. I was going to help people by being a mental health counselor. I convinced myself I was sacrificing a larger paycheck for the greater good. I used to rage over how little the "helping professions" got paid compared to business people, entertainers, and athletes. I didn't think it was fair. Here I was, motivated by my desire to help people, barely scraping by while the CEO of some big company, motivated by money, was making $20 million in stock options.

As I spent more time out in the real world, I started to understand just how twisted my thinking was. I wasn't some self-sacrificing altruist. Yes, I wanted to help people, but I also enjoyed being a mental health counselor. At the time it was what I wanted to do. I made that choice knowing what the salary was. There was nothing unfair about it. The salary was set by virtue of supply and demand for mental health counselors. And who did I think I was, reading everyone's minds on what their true motives were? What right did I have to think I'd cornered the market on compassion?

My belief that I could only make a lot of money if I betrayed my values was holding me back from achieving my dream. I had a belief that I would never make more than $30,000 or $40,000 a year. I didn't believe I could ever be financially rich *and* be a good person. That mindset made it very difficult for me to succeed. I didn't educate myself on how to invest because I would never have any money to invest with. I didn't think of starting my own business, because only rich people who made their money off their workers did that. I didn't work to find ways to make additional money with my skills because I never planned on making much.

It took me a long time, but I finally figured out you can do a lot of good in this world whether you're making $15,000 a year or $15 million a year. In fact, it could be argued that the more you make, the more good you are doing and can do. Once I realized that, it was a short leap to figure out *I* could help a lot more people, and myself, if I was making more money. What a revelation. It was as if scales had fallen from my eyes.

I started meeting nice, compassionate, rich people. They had always existed, I had just never been ready to see them before. In fact, one of the nicest men I have ever met is a multimillionaire. He was enjoying my radio show in Dallas one day and decided to give me a call. He invited me to a speech that was being given as part of the Tate Lecture Series at SMU. Later, he had me out to his house. He even introduced me to the vice president of the United States.

I could tell by talking to him that he had a very kind and compassionate heart. He would help people without expecting anything back or giving it a second thought. He was always asking what he could do for me. I tried to tell him he had already done more for me than he knew. He had completely shattered my old idea about rich people.

If you want to pursue your Passionate Purpose and achieve your ultimate success, including financial independence for yourself, you must get rid of the idea that money and rich people are inherently bad. And we must stop teaching our children that as well.

Serving Others

No one would remember the Good Samaritan if he'd only had good intentions; he had money as well.

–Margaret Thatcher, former prime minister of the United Kingdom

Beyond serving your fellow man with whatever goods or services you provide by pursuing your Passionate Purpose, your financial success will allow you to serve others in ways you never have before. The richer you get the more you can give. Won't it be great to start writing bigger checks to your favorite charities, causes, and churches?

Have you ever worked for someone poorer than you? I haven't. Have you ever been able to loan or give someone money when you were broke? I haven't. When you secure your financial future you get in the position where you can help so many others. That sure doesn't sound like the root of all evil to me.

Sometimes Money *Can* Buy Happiness

I've been rich and I've been poor—and believe me, rich is better.

–Attributed to Sophie Tucker, Pearl Bailey, Mae West, and others

Money can be a great motivator if it's for the right reason and doesn't become more important than the process you're using to earn it.

I've never been truly poor. I've never had to worry about having enough to eat. However, when my wife, Anne, and I were just starting out, we weren't making a lot of money. We had a couple things go wrong and we weren't exactly rolling in the dough.

I will never forget the day Anne called me crying. She's not overly emotional or given to crying at the drop of a hat, so I instantly thought something horrible had happened. She explained through tears that she was visiting our friends at the beach. She asked them if where she parked was OK and they said it was fine. Thirty minutes later, it wasn't fine. Anne felt horrible because she knew with our financial situation we couldn't afford to waste money.

It was a $12 parking ticket. That's it. Our income was so low that a $12 ticket was enough to make her cry. We laugh at that story now, but it reminds us that there is nothing great about being poor. It makes everything you want to do harder. It puts stress and worry on you that make your daily life hard.

People who say money can't buy happiness are right *and* wrong. I agree that trying to buy happiness by acquiring things is a fool's game. But if you don't think you're happier knowing you have enough money to eat and pay all the bills at the end of the month, you're crazy.

Some research asserts that, up to a point, as we earn more income our happiness increases. The debate is about the level where increased income no longer has a corresponding impact on our happiness. The latest studies I've seen claim the effect holds true until you reach the top 10 percent of earners.

In the book *Happy Money: The Science of Smarter Spending,* Elizabeth Dunn and Michael Norton explain some of the ways money really does buy happiness.

Buy Experiences

When we buy experiences instead of things the result is a bigger, long-lasting feeling of happiness. The memories from a fantastic trip to Europe will stick around much longer than the feeling you get from that new-car smell. You can tell those stories from your European trip for years and each time they will bring a smile to your face, especially if you made those memories with your friends or family.

There is a caveat, though. You need to buy the kind of experience that you actually like. I love going skiing. Spending money on a ski trip will definitely move me up the happiness scale. But I'm not a ballet or opera guy. If I get dragged to one of those events and I'm paying for it, not only will I not be happy, I'll probably be a bit grumpy.

Buy Time

Buying time increases your happiness. When we spend to keep our free time for what we want to do, that pays dividends. Paying for a maid service, for someone else to mow your lawn, or paying extra for your home or apartment in order to shorten your daily commute have all been shown to move you up on the happy scale.

Give It Away

Some research shows that when you give as little as five dollars to a charity, or to someone who needs it, your happiness level goes up more than when you spend it on yourself. I know that's true for me. I still feel good about a small thing I did years ago. A friend of ours was going through a divorce. She had no money to hire an attorney and had no clue how to handle everything she was going through. Anne and I were doing well enough that we were able to give her the money to get the professional help she needed. It felt great at the time to help out a friend and I still feel good every time I remember it. If Anne and I weren't earning more than enough to take care of ourselves, we couldn't have helped her.

Giving away your money for happiness doesn't just work when you give to charities, churches, or people who really need it. Believe it or not, picking up the tab when you go out with your buddies gives you a little jolt of happiness. (And I'm willing to allow you that happiness if we ever go out for drinks together.)

Think back to a time you donated to a good cause or a friend who needed help. Still feels good, doesn't it? Make it a goal to increase your giving and increase everyone's happiness.

I'm tired of hearing people bad mouth the idea of becoming wealthy. Most people do not become rich by exploiting others or by acting like jerks. Most people make more money the more they serve others. That's a good thing for everybody.

I like not having to worry about where my next meal is coming from, don't you? That's a start, but I like to take inspiring vacations with my family and make lifelong memories. I enjoy living in a beautiful home and eating out at nice restaurants. It's a wonderful feeling to be in a position where you are able to donate to your church, charities, and people in your neighborhood. Making more money isn't just OK, it can be what allows you to do all the other things you've been dreaming about.

Change Your Body Language and Change Your Attitude

You've probably heard the expression "Fake it until you make it." Did you know there is actually research that backs that up?

It's virtually impossible to feel deeply depressed when you take on the body posture and facial expressions of someone who just scored their dream job or who just won the lottery. Try it.

To see how true this is you need to spend two to three minutes really acting it out. Imagine you just inherited five million dollars. How would you stand? Would you be slumped over or erect? Would you jump up and down? Pump your fist? Scream? Hold both arms up? How big would your smile be? Would your muscles be tight or slack? Really get into it and let your body and face do what they would do if you had truly just come into that much cash.

Hold that posture and that feeling. Now, feel as sad as you possibly can. Get sad. Right now. If you were able to change your positive feelings to negative ones that quickly, how do you look? Did your body posture change? Did you facial expressions change? I bet they did. It's virtually impossible to feel sad and look ecstatic at the same time.

Try it the opposite way as well. Can you feel like you're on top of the world while you're slouched down in a chair with the most depressed body posture you can imagine and a facial expression that says your favorite dog just died? Not really.

That's why, sometimes, it pays to "fake it until you make it." Yes, you can sometimes shake yourself out of a small funk by walking, talking, and smiling as if you're happy and ready to take on the day.

This doesn't mean that we are constantly pretending we're happy no matter what. That would be insane and cause you other problems. We need to deal with issues that are dragging us down and fix real problems we have. But the more you emulate what a positive, happy, optimistic person looks like, the more you actually will become one.

Amy Cuddy has given a great Ted Talk on her research on this. She found that our body postures can even change our hormones. When people in her research performed one of the "power poses" for as little as two minutes, their testosterone levels increased 20 percent and their stress cortisol levels decreased 25 percent. These positions made the participants feel more powerful and confident. What's more, neutral observers who did not know which people had done the power poses rated the people who had done them as more powerful than the ones who had not practiced them. It seems your body doesn't understand that you're just faking it.

But wait, there's more.

Erik Pepper's behavioral science research shows that how we sit, stand, and move impacts our energy levels and how we feel. When we sit up straight, it's easier to think positive thoughts. When we've been sitting for a while, getting up to stretch, skip, and "wiggle" boosts our energy levels and our ability to concentrate.

This type of research has been around since the late 1800s, so isn't it time you took advantage of it?

It's All About Your Mindset

Your mindset is essential to your success. When you understand you earn more when you serve more, you can feel good about your efforts and your progress. You know you are providing goods and services to people that are enriching their lives. They joyfully line up to give you money for your efforts because you are providing great value. You are one of the good guys!

When you believe there is infinite wealth to be created in this life you don't need to look at everyone else as competition. You can truly be happy for other people's achievements because you know it does absolutely nothing to diminish your chance of being successful and might even *help* you succeed. There is more than enough for us all.

How can we get more people on the path to pursuing their Passionate Purpose? First we have to get people into the mindset that this is the kind of life we were meant to live. God didn't create us just to get by. God created us to be fruitful and multiply. He created us to turn one talent into ten and use the gifts he gave us. He created us to have an abundant life so that we can help others who don't have as much. He created us to live a life full of joy. Until you believe that, you will subconsciously sabotage any attempt to pursue your Passionate Purpose.

Your new mindset starts with re-educating yourself. You have to undue all the nonsense about how life is "supposed to be" that was drilled into you growing up. Let's begin with what you wanted to be. The answer is no longer the title of your job. The belief that you are your job has held countless Americans back from true success and enjoyment in their lives. You do not equal your job. You are much more than that. You have to know who you are, what you stand for and what you *want* in every phase of your life.

I am a: Christian, man, husband, father, son, brother, musician, surfer, singer, talk show host, speaker, author, investor, blogger, video maker, webmaster, friend, cook, traveler, and adventure seeker who has unique goals for every part of my life.

Remember, the questions you ask yourself create your focus, feelings, and actions. Who are you? Who do you want to be? What do you *want?* If you still aren't sure and still don't have your specific goals written down, go back to the chapters that walk you through this. Think deeply about these questions and answer them as completely as you can for your life.

Who are you spiritually and physically? Who are you as a spouse, child, parent, sibling, friend, employee, entrepreneur, and wealth creator? Who do you *want* to be? What do you *want* your family, friends, co-workers, and strangers to say about you when you're gone? While you're here?

Your answers to these questions can help you create your own personal manifesto or mission statement. It will be your guide on what matters to you and how to get to your goals while keeping faith with your values.

As Stephen Covey says in the *Seven Habits of Highly Effective People*, that's what our founding fathers did with our country. The Constitution was their guide on exactly what this country was, what it stood for, and what they hoped it would be.

The United States Constitution set our country up to be the perfect breeding ground for this type of life. Our rights are outlined as being endowed on us by our Creator. No man, no president, no king, no government can take these rights from us. The entire document is about limiting the power of government and protecting the inalienable rights of the individual. Pursuing your Passionate Purpose is the dream of our founders. We need to develop a constitution for our lives and teach our children to do the same for theirs.

What's your Mission Statement for your life? Spend some time figuring it out as if you were a corporation. Write it down. Read it every morning and night. Everything you do should be in line with that Mission Statement.

Once you know who you are, what you stand for, and what you *want*, you are ready to outline your customized Passionate Purpose in every phase of your life (If you haven't already done so earlier in the book, stop and do this right now. Don't put it off. I'm talking to you. Put down the book and do it right *now*.)

Your goals won't be the same as mine. Everyone has different dreams. Don't get caught up in comparing your life to what society says is success. It's not about anyone else but you.

> *Winners compare their achievements with their goals, while losers compare their achievements with those of other people.*
>
> –Nido Qubein, businessman and motivational speaker

Obstacles

> *Obstacles are those frightful things you see when you take your eyes off your goals.*
>
> –Henry Ford

As soon as you decide on your Passionate Purpose and set goals, obstacles arise. Two big obstacles can hold you back from pursuing this new American dream if you let them. The first one can be an obstacle or an ally. It is your mindset. You must develop a new mindset and change the way you think about success, failure, security, risk, money, income, wealth, poverty, relationships, work, luck, and more. You will need a new attitude and a new outlook on life to get everything you want.

The second obstacle that can derail your success is fear. But don't despair. We can even turn fear into an ally.

Techniques from the Masters

- A positive attitude and mindset is crucial in pursuing your Passionate Purpose.
- Start every morning thinking about all the things you're grateful for in your life.
- Make your default body language mirror someone who is having a great day. Remember, how we sit, stand, and move impacts how we feel and our energy levels.
- Eliminate any negative beliefs about success and successful people.
- Strive to succeed while living by the Golden Rule. Become a benevolent millionaire.
- Remember what Zig Ziglar said. "You can get everything in life you want if you will just help enough other people get what they want."
- Choose your friends wisely. Create a peer group of people who are also on the journey of pursuing their Passionate Purpose.
- Celebrate other people's successes.

Pleasure and Pain

How to Use Pleasure and Pain to Pursue
Your Passionate Purpose

The secret of success is learning how to use pain and pleasure instead of having pain and pleasure use you. If you do that, you're in control of your life. If you don't, life controls you.

–Anthony Robbins, author and motivational speaker

When I hear something that makes sense, I pay attention. When I hear it from someone else in a different way a second time, I start studying it. When I hear it a third time and it relates to my personal experiences I become a true believer. That's what happened to me with the idea of how we are all motivated by two things: pleasure and pain.

Greg, you've gone crazy again. I am motivated by a lot more than that. I'm motivated by love, money, significance, my values, friends, my family, joy, anger, negative circumstances … I'm motivated by a lot more than pleasure and pain.

Easy, tiger. I'm not trying to get you upset. But stop and think for a second. Pick something, anything, that motivates your behavior. Let's use money. Why do you want more money? Lots of reasons, right? To take care of your family, to pay your bills, to secure your future, to buy your dream house, to take your family on wonderful vacations and build dreams together. Don't all those reasons really boil down to increasing your pleasure?

Now what happens if you lose the ability to earn a good income? You will lose your home, you won't be able to feed your family or pay for your children to go to college. Your spouse might leave you (hopefully that's an irrational fear, but a real one nonetheless), you will feel like a failure, you may end up on welfare. Don't all those answers boil down to increasing your pain?

We are all motivated by our desire for pleasure and our fear of pain. When we alter the way we think and act to use pleasure and pain to our advantage we can transform our lives.

Fear

Never let the fear of striking out get in your way.

–Babe Ruth, baseball player

Questions can be very powerful. What you ask yourself changes what you focus on. What you focus on determines how you feel and what actions you will take. One of the big questions we're asked time and again is about our jobs.

When we were young, all of us were asked by adults, "What do you want to be when you grow up?" We were trained by our parents, our friends, our schools, and society that the question really meant, "What job do you want when you grow up?" The answer changed as we aged. As a little child the answer was fireman, cowboy, ballerina, nurse, or teacher. As we got older the answer was doctor, lawyer, engineer, businessman, entrepreneur, teacher, mother, father, or inventor. Very few of us ever answered "mid-management assistant to the director." Unfortunately, that's the job a lot of us settled for.

We were taught that if we got that "good job" and worked hard for 40-60 hours a week, 50 weeks a year, we would have a "secure income." That traditional idea of how to earn money and provide for your family has been burned into our psyche. Many of us have never dreamed there was another way. When we hear people talk about a new way, we reject it outright. One of the reasons we reject it is fear.

Sometimes it helps to get mugged by reality. An increasing number of Americans are starting to understand there is no "security." No matter where you work, there is no guarantee you won't be laid off two weeks from now. The old American dream is done. Stick a fork in it.

Could there actually be a positive side to this? Yes. Having the old American dream shattered can open your mind to the idea that there is a better way. It's time to ask new questions. In terms of your career, what do you want to do with your life? What can you do to earn a great income and have fun at the same time? Where do you want to go? What's your passion?

When you pursue your Passionate Purpose the rewards are limited only by your imagination, determination, and hard work. It sounds great, so who wouldn't want it? What holds so many people back?

This is a totally new, radical idea for the vast majority of Americans. It's scary. It has ups and downs. It requires a lot of hard work. There is fear in the unknown. When people start to seriously consider finding and pursuing their Passionate Purpose, fear creeps in.

Some of these fears are rational and some are irrational. Fear is a very powerful emotion. It can paralyze you if you let it.

Fear of failing

Fear of pain

Fear of letting your family down

Fear of divorce if you fail

Fear of rejection

Fear of losing all your money

Fear of looking stupid

Fear that you're not smart enough or good enough

Fear of losing everything you've worked so hard for in your life

That's just a partial list. What are you afraid of that is holding you back from committing to and pursuing your Passionate Purpose? What is subservience to this fear costing you?

> *I'd rather be a failure at something I love than a success at something I hate.*
>
> –George Burns, comedian, actor

I will never forget a decision I made in eighth grade. I wanted to try out for our junior high baseball team. I was a really good infielder and even though I didn't hit for power, I usually put the ball in play. But all the "cool guys" were on the baseball team. I was definitely not a "cool guy." I was what you would call a dork. I was skinny, short, wore glasses and my brother's hand-me-downs. I got picked on by the cool guys. I was petrified that I would embarrass myself at the tryouts.

Even though I usually played shortstop or third base, I signed up to try out in the outfield. My reasoning was the best players were the infielders and I doubted I was good enough. My fear got so bad that on the day of tryouts I didn't go. I just went home on the bus. I still regret it to this day.

Don't let your fears stop you from pursuing your passions. Try it. Do it. Ask for it. As my dad always says, the answer is already "no" until you ask. They might say yes. What have you got to lose?

Friends and Family Who Mean Well Will Feed Your Fear

As you get close to starting one of these new ventures, fear will start creeping in. You will start questioning yourself. Am I smart enough to do this? Can I really make money at this? What happens if I lose it all? What happens if I fail? Am I just wasting my time? I have asked myself every one of those questions, and at times I still do. Please don't think you're the only one who has these doubts.

Everyone who has ever pursued a dream has had fear and doubt creep in during their journey. What separates the successful is that they persevered and pushed through those feelings. They realized they were temporary and necessary hurdles to overcome to get to where they wanted to go and to become who they wanted to be. If they could do it, you can do it, too.

It helps if you pick your friends wisely. You want to surround yourself with people who want you to succeed and people who are also pursuing excellence. Most of us will only rise as high as the people in our peer group. If you look around and you are the most successful person in your group, you need to find some new friends. I know that sounds harsh, but it's true. That doesn't mean you have to cut ties with everyone else, but it does mean you need to make sure that they aren't pulling you down or lowering your standards for who you want to be and what you want to achieve.

Unfortunately, some of your friends and family will feed those fears. Some of them will do it because they love you and think they are helping you avoid a big mistake. Others will do it because they are not willing to pursue their Passionate Purpose themselves and resent the fact that you are doing what they don't have the courage or commitment to do. There's a little jealousy and envy inside them that doesn't want you to succeed. Sometimes they're not even self-aware enough to realize that's what they're doing. But somewhere in their brain is the nagging question, if you are succeeding and they aren't, what does that say about them? They will have to question themselves and how they are living their life. That is very uncomfortable. If comparing themselves to you makes them feel bad, they may even make up stories about how you succeeded that aren't very nice. It's sad, but I bet it will happen to you.

This is another reason for you to practice celebrating other people's successes. You don't want to be a drag on your friends or family, do you? This will make you a better friend. More people will want to be part of your peer group. It will come back to you in so many great ways and you will feel much better than being envious or jealous of other people living out their dreams.

Remember, when you tell yourself that someone only reached their goal be being greedy, or mean, or by exploiting others you will actually be making it harder to achieve your own success. If being successful equals being a horrible person, why would you want to be successful? It goes back to the mindset we discussed earlier.

You can't pick your family, but you can pick your friends. Love your family, but avoid talking about your dreams with the dream killers. Pick your friends wisely and be the kind of friend who encourages, supports, and celebrates with others when they succeed.

Use Fear to Your Advantage

Don't be afraid to go out on a limb. That's where the fruit is.

–H. Jackson Browne, author

So how do you fight this powerful fear and negative talk from yourself and others? You fight it with a great purpose, courage, *another* fear, good preparation and planning, and a positive mindset. We're going to use the Christmas Carol technique.

If you take this exercise seriously and fully commit to it, you can use fear to your advantage and lock in your focus to your new Passionate Purpose. I learned this one from Anthony Robbins years ago. I still use it to maintain my motivation anytime I start to think things are getting too hard. This exercise helps you elevate the pain you will feel if you give into your fears and then elevate the pleasure you will feel by pursuing your Passionate Purpose.

To do this right, you should spend a good fifteen minutes going deep into your thoughts and feelings to make it seem as real as possible. If you've ever seen Charles Dickens' *A Christmas Carol,* you'll have a pretty good idea of what you should be trying to do.

I normally only focus these types of exercises on the positive outcomes you want in your life. I am a big believer in whatever we focus on, we get more of. So why would you want to focus on feeling possible negative outcomes in your life? When done correctly, this exercise is so powerful I am willing to break my rule. However, I only want you to do this once. From then on we are going to turn this same technique into focusing on positive outcomes.

Imagine what your life will be like if you do not change to follow what you were created to do. If you're lucky, you will bounce from job to job chasing the paycheck to take care of your family. You'll invest some money in your 401(k) and hope and pray it won't go down right around the time you're trying to retire. You will go to work every day with a feeling deep inside you that you aren't doing what you were put on this earth to do. You will spend 40-60 hours a week doing a job you don't like, or maybe even hate.

Close your eyes and think about doing this job you hate and all the things in your life that bother you. Imagine this is as good as it will ever get. Imagine all the dreams you have dying unfulfilled. You never get that dream job, never pursue that Passionate Purpose burning inside you, never make more money, never get closer to your loved ones, never travel to new places, never improve your relationship with God, never help the people you care about, never move into your dream home.

You never ________________________.

You never grow. You never change. You're stuck like this until the day you die. Imagine that you don't do anything we've talked about in this book. You do nothing different so nothing changes a year from now. What would that feel like? What would it look like? What would it sound, smell, and taste like? Does that scare you? Does that create emotional pain for you?

Now imagine nothing has changed and it's *five years* from now. You keep doing the same things every day. You're no closer to your dreams and goals than you were five years ago, but you're five years older. You're going through the motions 40 to 60 hours a week. Sunday after Sunday you dread the following Monday. You live for the weekends and two measly weeks a year of vacation—if you're lucky. But it pays the bills and you're doing "OK." *Years* go by and you feel like the life is being sucked out of you. You aren't the fun-loving, optimistic person you used to be. Your kids and spouse aren't getting the best of you anymore. You realize sometimes you are taking out your frustrations on them. You feel depressed with where your life is. You keep putting off the things you know you should do and you get angry with yourself for not following through. Your self-esteem keeps sinking lower. How does that feel? Is it painful yet?

Now do it again and project your life out ten years, twenty years. Think about your life with no growth and no changes *thirty* years from now. Make it as real as you can and feel it right now. Spend five to ten minutes really feeling this. I'll wait. …

(Man this kettle corn microwave popcorn is really good! Oh, you're back. Hey!)

OK, how scary are those feelings?

And what if becoming stagnant where you are is the *best-case* scenario. What happens if your company lays you off? What happens if the job you do becomes obsolete? What happens if you don't work on your marital relationship and that leads to divorce?

See, I think it's scarier *not* to change than it is to take the risk of trying something new. You're either growing or dying. Which one sounds better to you?

Do you want to be just one of the masses where everybody's working for the weekend? It was a hit for the band Loverboy for a reason, but last time I checked, the weekend is only two out of every seven days. Gee, let's struggle through five lousy days for two good ones and then start the miserable cycle over again for the next 60 years. Then we can lie on our deathbed wondering what might have been.

> *Oh, you hate your job? Why didn't you say so? There's a support group for that. It's called* everybody, *and they meet at the bar.*
>
> –Drew Carey, comedian, actor

Sound like fun? Sound like success? Do you think that won't affect the rest of your life negatively? Are you a fun parent or spouse to be around when all you do is put your dreams on pause and hold on until the weekend comes? I don't know about you, but *that's* what I'm afraid of.

It's arguable that the new American dream of pursuing your Passionate Purpose is less risky than the old one. It certainly has more potential rewards.

> *Twenty years from now you will be more disappointed by the things that you didn't do than by the ones you did do. So throw off the bowlines. Sail away from the safe harbor. Catch the trade winds in your sails. Explore. Dream. Discover.*
>
> –Mark Twain

Imagining how your life could go if you don't pursue your passion is pretty powerful, isn't it? It scares the mess out of me. It's a great motivator for me. I am scared to death of living a boring life, of waking up on my last day with a long list of regrets and what ifs. Dying with a fire in your heart that you never let the world see would be the ultimate, final tragedy of your life.

That fear we just created is greater than the fear I might fail at following my Passionate Purpose. If you approach this as if you can't afford to fail, as if your future depends on it, you will succeed. You may stumble a couple of times as you begin your pursuit, but every time you do you will learn something, you will become something better than you are right now, and you will be one step closer to succeeding the next time.

> *"Come to the edge," he said.*
> *"We can't, we're afraid!" they responded.*
> *"Come to the edge," he said.*
> *"We can't, We will fall!" they responded.*
> *"Come to the edge," he said.*
> *And so they came.*
> *And he pushed them.*
> *And they flew.*
>
> –Guillaume Apollinaire, poet, playwright, short-story writer, novelist, and art critic

Use Pleasure to Your Advantage

Now that I've led you through an exercise that scared the life out of you (you're welcome, by the way) let's not stop there. We need to use the other part of the equation as well. We agreed that we are motivated to avoid pain and increase pleasure. We just got intimate with how painful our fear of a wasted life is. Now let's get a deep emotional feeling of how much pleasure the life of our dreams could be.

Do the Christmas Carol exercise again. But this time think about what your life will be like when you start pursuing your Passionate Purpose every day. What will you have accomplished and what kind of a person will you be one year from now? Write down every good thing you can about what that would be like. What will you be earning an income doing? What will your family life be like? What will your physical and spiritual fitness be? How eager will you be to jump out of bed each morning? How much more freedom to pursue your desires will you have? How great will it feel to be highly valued for what you are contributing to others? Visualize what your life will be like. Feel the feelings that come with that life.

Now do the same exercise for imagining your extraordinary life five years from now. What have you achieved already and what are you pursuing now? How big an income are you generating? What kind of home are you living in? How have you improved your most important relationships even more? How has every area of your life improved? What are you most thankful for now? Go deep into your imagination. Feel the emotions well up inside you.

Everyone Can Do This

Hold it, Greg. I can't do this. I'm not a good pretender. I can't visualize. This doesn't work for me.

OK. Let's relax for a second and I think I can help.

Hey, I just saw a purple elephant with wings fly over my house! It was the size of a school bus and it was making that crazy elephant noise!

I'm betting your brain just created a picture of a huge, purple elephant with wings flying over a house. Your brain may have even created a sound in your head that the elephant made. Guess what. You just pretended and visualized. We do it every day. Everyone can do it. The more you do it the better you get at it.

The word pretend could make you feel like a child, but it's not just a silly kids game. If it makes you feel better call it visualizing instead. We visualize all the time. If we pretend things are awful and visualize negative outcomes, that hurts us. If we visualize positive outcomes, that helps us.

How many times have you told yourself things like, "this won't work" and "I'm going to get fired?" Aren't you pretending you know what's going to happen? Aren't you visualizing the future? What about when you plan your big vacation to the Bahamas? As you look at the websites of the beautiful beach resorts and schedule when you're going to go snorkeling, aren't you pretending what it's going to be like and visualizing how great and relaxing the time with your family will be?

When you feel totally prepared for a big project or presentation at work don't you visualize how well it's going to turn out? You may not even notice you're doing it, but it has a big impact on your mood, your confidence, and your performance.

All we're doing here is consciously creating the visualization of the life we want to lead. We are creating a great desire inside us for the pleasure we know will come as we pursue our Passionate Purpose. Does that make sense?

I bet you can imagine how your life would change if you won the $200 million Powerball lottery, right? OK, that's basically what we're doing here.

Let's get back into the Christmas Carol technique again and really get to the emotional level this time. Use the same prompts about your life we have been using and look out ten years. Now 15 years. Now 20 years. How extraordinary is your life now? Visualize achieving every goal you have for the next 20 years of your life. Everything you've ever wanted to do, be, learn, earn, and give has come to pass. Your relationships are better than you thought possible. You walk with your Creator. You are giving abundantly to the people and causes you believe in. You are living in your dream home and taking vacations around the world with your loved ones and making priceless memories. See it, feel it, and experience it as if it has already happened. Get deep into it. Convince yourself it's real.

How do you feel right now? You're welcome.

See It, Feel It, Do It

Every day when you read your goals spend five minutes seeing, feeling, and experiencing your goals as if you've already achieved them. This will keep you motivated and trigger your subconscious to work on your path to your goals even while you sleep. I know it sounds kind of out there. Test it out for a month and see what happens. The worst that happens is you feel really good for five minutes a day. But I am confident you will get so much out this daily exercise that it will become a new habit in your life.

Techniques from the Masters

- We are all motivated by our desire for pleasure and our fear of pain. When we alter the way we think and act to use pleasure and pain to our advantage we can transform our lives.

- What you ask yourself changes what you focus on. What you focus on determines how you feel and what actions you will take. Ask yourself questions that get you positively focused on what you want.

- Understand that fear is normal and can be good or bad.

- Use the Christmas Carol technique in order to use *fear* to your advantage.

- Use the Christmas Carol technique in order to use *pleasure* to your advantage.

- Make it a daily habit to spend at least five minutes visualizing your goals. Feel, see, and experience them as if you have already achieved them.

Focus

A Laser Focus Gets You There Faster

The successful man is the average man, focused.

–Anonymous

Multitasking Doesn't Help and Doesn't Exist

Do you ever feel overwhelmed? Is there too much to do and too little time? Are you spending all your time putting out fires instead of pursuing your Passionate Purpose and achieving your goals?

Does a one-legged duck swim in circles?

Yes, thank you, Captain Obvious. We're all busy and trying to do a million things. What's your point?

(Get ready, big insight coming …)

You can't do it all. You certainly can't do it all well. You can't even enjoy *trying* to do it all. So why do we insist on trying? Why do we feel guilty when we fail?

It reminds me of the old commercial where a pretty young woman sang, "I can bring home the bacon, fry it up in a pan, and never let you forget you're a man, cause I'm a woman …"

Talk about pressure. Can anyone do all that every day? Does anyone want to? We've been fed this nonsense that if you don't do that, you're lazy. Or inadequate. Or a loser.

But wait, we can put even more ridiculous pressure on you. Not only should you put more on your to-do list than you can possibly do, you need to do several of the tasks at the same time.

We are told to be more productive we must multitask. We can catch up on our email while we're in our morning sales meeting. Or we can talk to customers on the phone while typing up a report that's due at the end of the day.

Numerous studies show there is no such thing as multitasking. We are never truly doing two things at once. What we really do is quickly switch back and forth between the two or three tasks we are *trying* to do at the same time. Our brain will focus on the customer on the phone while pulling away from the report. Then it will quickly shift back to the report and pull away from focusing on the call. We end up doing a mediocre job at both and taking longer to complete the tasks. But we might feel like we were more productive.

Even computers don't truly multitask. When you have three or four applications running on your computer they are not all running at once. The processor is switching between the three tasks multiple times every second. It gives the appearance that it's getting done quicker and simultaneously, but it isn't.

Why do we keep trying to do something even the computer can't do?

> *To do two things at once is to do neither.*
>
> –Publilius Syrus, Latin writer and former slave

With the advent of smart phones, text messaging, email, email attachments, pdf files, digital signatures and more, we are told that everything has to be responded to, done, and sent … right NOW!

How has that worked out for us? We are busier than ever, more stressed than ever, and more scattered than ever. Is this what we want?

This lack of focus on what's truly important in our day doesn't lead to getting our top priorities done well. It doesn't lead to a great feeling at the end of the day that we accomplished something, or we've created art, or pursued our passion. It leaves us drained and discontented. It leaves us saying we have too much work and too little time.

> *Lack of direction, not lack of time, is the problem. We all have twenty-four-hour days.*
>
> –Zig Ziglar

It's really not our fault, we all have ADHD now, right? Attention Deficit Hyperactivity Disorder has become an epidemic, a slang term and an excuse. Yes, there really are people who have ADHD. It's a real thing. But when most of us say we didn't finish something because of our ADHD, what we're really saying is we couldn't, or wouldn't, stay focused.

Focusing on the most important thing we need to do is the key to a productive, rewarding day. If we stay focused on our top priority and block out all other distractions, tiny miracles start to happen. It seems like we have more time, not less. We are more relaxed and less hurried. We are more creative and think deeper. We come up with original solutions to problems.

You've had days where your focus was sharp haven't you? Those were great days, right? So why don't we set up a system to make all our days like that?

Get Focused and Stay Focused

Now that you've discovered what you're passionate about, go after it with a laser focus. Go after that one thing with all your spare time. Read books about it. Attend seminars on it. Get a mentor who has already become successful at it. Become an expert. If you put one or two hours a night into one thing, you will be surprised how quickly you will come to know it well.

If this is the new career for you, take that focus and find multiple ways to generate income from it.

Here's how it works for me: I enjoy speaking, teaching, writing, performing, and sharing my ideas on discovering and pursuing your Passionate Purpose. I am able to use that expertise to generate income from books, training seminars, speaking events, DVDs, audiobooks, and eBooks. It all adds up to numerous income sources from one Passionate Purpose.

I'm an analytical guy and I read a ton before I do anything. That can be good, but it can also lead to the dreaded "paralysis by analysis." I sometimes research and plan to the point that I never actually do it.

> *Nothing will ever be attempted if all possible objections must first be overcome.*
>
> –Samuel Johnson, poet, essayist, moralist, literary critic, and biographer

A friend of mine said something to me that keeps me pressing forward even when I'm not 100 percent sure how to do everything I will need to know how to do before my project is finished. He said, "Greg, when you leave here to go home tonight are you going to sit in your car until all the streetlights from here to your house turn green? No, you're going to drive up to the first red light and wait for it to turn green. Then you're going to drive to the next red light. You're going to keep doing that until you get home. That's how it is with the new ventures you're working on now. If you wait until you have every detail planned from now until the end, you will never start."

That doesn't mean that you don't prepare or you go off half-cocked without a plan. It does mean that you don't wait for everything to be perfect before you start moving. You set out a rough plan and begin. You go until you hit an obstacle and then you find a way around it and move on to the next one, and then the next one. Before you know it, you're doing it.

Pick one area and focus on it. Then, GO! A goal is just a daydream until you take action to make it become a reality. You will make mistakes, hit brick walls, fall down, and get discouraged. That's OK. Just keep going. Failure is never permanent unless you choose to let it be. There is no straight line up to success.

The people with perseverance are the most successful people in the world. That's why it's so important to pursue your Passionate Purpose and not just some job you think will make you a lot of money. No matter how much you make, if you hate your job you will eventually be miserable. If you're doing work you enjoy, it will steel you against the hard times and keep you motivated as you surpass one obstacle after another.

If you are spending 40-60 hours a week on something, doesn't it make sense to make it something you enjoy and are passionate about? So find it, focus, and GO!

Once you've got that area going strong, work on ways to expand your sources of income from there. But the tortoise is still right. Slow and steady wins the race.

One Thing at a Time

Gary Keller and Jay Papasan's book, *The ONE Thing*, has some great techniques on how to stay focused on your goals and priorities every day.

Keller and Papasan suggest you begin each day with this question:

"What's the ONE Thing you can do such that by doing it everything else will be easier or unnecessary?"

It's a powerful question. It keeps you focused. It helps you spend your energy where it matters most. One of the strategies in the book is to block out four hours each day to concentrate on your ONE Thing. Let everyone know what you're doing and why. Be protective of that time. That means no checking emails or social media. It means no meetings or talking with a co-worker about the game last night. This is your supreme focus time. Yes, you will still need to take breaks during this time, but not to start down the road of distractions and time-killers.

In an interview with Forbes, Keller put it this way, "Think of it like going to the movies. You're there for ONE Thing—to see the film. Because you're really clear about that, you turn off your cell phone, you grab snacks in case you get hungry, and you probably even make a pit stop before you go in. All this so you can have an uninterrupted experience.

"When you time block your most important work and treat it like going to the movies—you make a stand around avoiding distractions—amazing things happen. When you start thinking of your days this way, the burden of always having to be 'on' goes away and you end up accomplishing more."

You will have to get creative on how you block out that time. Make sure everyone who needs to know understands why you are doing this. Your boss and you colleagues will be very happy when they start to see the increased creativity and productivity in your work. If you are the boss, or you're self-employed, you are going to be shocked at how much more of the important stuff you get done when you start focusing four hours a day on the ONE Thing.

More Than One Focus

OK, Greg, that sounds pretty cool, but I have more than one thing I want to do in life. I have more than one goal.

Good! I would hope so. Just because you are focused on one thing right now doesn't mean that you only have one thing you care about. The point is that success comes by doing ONE Thing … and then doing another ONE Thing, and then another. Regardless of what Oprah tells us, we can't do more than one thing at a time. So focus, do the ONE Thing, and then do the next thing.

You can even alternate what ONE Thing you are focusing on from day to day. The key, though, is the focus. While you're working on one goal, don't let your mind drift to the next one. Do your ONE Thing with all your effort and do it well. You will be amazed by how much more you accomplish and how much more quickly.

A Healthy Dose of Vitamin N

Focusing is about saying No.

–Steve Jobs, entrepreneur, marketer, and inventor who was the co-founder, chairman, and CEO of Apple Inc.

One of the easiest ways to get distracted is to say yes too much. We all want to be the "team player." We don't want to be called selfish, lazy, or rude. We want to say yes to our boss when she asks us to take on another project. We want to say yes to our colleagues who ask us for help.

But will that help us get where we want to go? Is that the way to do our best work? Every time we say yes to what someone else wants from us, we are also saying no to time focused on *our own* goals and what *we* want. If we're spread too thin trying to help everyone with their work we will end up with poor results for them and for the work we are *supposed* to be doing.

We need to administer a healthy dose of vitamin N every day. We need to be comfortable saying, "No." We can be nice in how we say no, but we don't need to act like we're doing something horrible by saying no, either.

Here are some ways to say no:

- Thanks for asking me, but I'm in the middle of a project right now that I need to finish by my deadline.
- I'm not the best person to help on this one. That's really Jim's specialty.

- I've already committed to X right now. I know you will do a great job.
- I'm not able to set aside the time needed to do that well.
- I'm honored you thought of me, but I'm not able to help on this one.
- No, I'm not able to do that.

It will take some practice getting good at saying no, but it will change your life. Try it out. See how it feels. Say no to someone today. Say no to two people tomorrow. It is liberating.

We have a special rule on the smart phone at the Knapp house. Here it is:

"The phone is for our convenience, not for the caller's."

Just because someone calls, texts, or emails you doesn't mean you have to answer it. You didn't ask them to contact you and you are not required to immediately answer them. We don't even look at the phone during dinner and family time. Later, we decide if, and when, we will return a call.

Does this sound rude to you? I used to feel that way. But another way to look at it is, would you let someone walk in your house or place of business and demand that you immediately meet their needs? Wouldn't you call *that* rude?

This isn't to suggest that you always say no, or that you never help out a co-worker or a friend. This isn't carte blanche permission to say no to everyone. You will still say yes to your spouse, kids, boss, church, etc., but you won't say it all the time.

The point is that you are strategic as to when you say yes and you make sure that no is not a dirty word. It will end up helping you, and everyone you care about, more than saying yes to all comers.

Maybe you're like me. I have ten ideas a day on cool stuff that I would like to do. If I spent my time jumping from one to the other, I'd never finish anything. I struggle with this quite a bit.

I have my job as a talk radio host where I spend four hours on the air every day and at least four hours prepping for the show. I am writing this book. I run a blog. I give speeches. I make short videos. I play guitar. I have a family. I am trying to be more active in my church. I am helping my youngest daughter publish her book.

We have to focus to get anything done. I finally learned my lesson on this when I got frustrated in my efforts to become a better guitar player.

There are countless ways to play the guitar: fingerstyle, classical, rock, blues, country, blue grass, jazz, and on and on. I could also focus on playing rhythm or lead. I would love to be great at all these styles. But that isn't my full-time job. I finally figured out that with the limited time I have, I can become mediocre at all of these, or I can become pretty good at two or three. Since I love to play and sing in my band, I decided to focus on becoming a really good rhythm guitar player. I still dabble in playing lead for fun, but my ONE Thing on guitar is rhythm.

It's the same for other parts of my life. Quite often I have three or four big projects I'm working on, plus my day job. I can't block out four hours every day for each one. But I can focus on ONE Thing and make some big progress.

Give it a try and see what happens.

> *The key to success is to focus our conscious mind on things we desire not things we fear.*
>
> –Brian Tracy, author and speaker

Techniques from the Masters

- There is no such thing as multitasking. You will end up doing multiple things poorly. Don't even try it.
- Focus on the ONE Thing. Ask this question: "What's the ONE Thing you can do such that by doing it everything else will be easier or unnecessary?"
- Block out four hours a day to focus on your ONE Thing.
- Your main focus can change from day to day, but don't change your main focus from moment to moment.
- Practice saying no to the things that take you away from your goals and what you want to accomplish.

Victims Will Never Live Out Their Passionate Purpose

How to Take Control of Your Past and Your Circumstances

Definition of a victim: a person to whom life happens.

–Peter McWilliams, author

Nothing can stop you from living out your Passionate Purpose faster than believing you are a victim. Everything that goes along with being a victim is in direct conflict with what you need to succeed. When you see yourself as a victim you are helpless, hopeless, depressed, self-pitying, blaming, negative, and unlovable. Other than that, it's a gay old time.

We've all been through times when we felt like the victim. I still have times where I throw myself a pity party. Because even though victimhood holds us back from moving forward to the success we want, it also holds rewards for us.

It's a lot easier playing the victim than taking responsibility for our own life and working hard to achieve something. It can also be a great excuse. But that small pleasure and avoidance of working on fixing our problems comes with a huge cost.

Once you believe you're a victim at the mercy of circumstances, what's the point in trying? You are not in control of your own destiny, so why put in the hard work it takes to change, grow, and achieve what you want? If you have no power to change your life you're doomed to whatever life, other people, chance, or fate does to you.

Gee, sign me up for that life. That sounds super.

Victims Will Never Live Out Their Passionate Purpose

Your victimhood can be real or imagined, but no matter what bad hand life has dealt you, the beginning of your way out is knowing and believing that you control what happens to you from this point forward. Once you believe that, you have a chance. Now you have the beginning of the motivation necessary to change your life forever.

The greatest part of our happiness depends on our dispositions, not our circumstances.

–Martha Washington, First Lady of the United States

Short, Slow, and Couldn't Jump

I loved basketball. I was pretty good at it. The more I played, the more I started dreaming about winning a college scholarship and maybe even playing in the NBA. The competition got stiffer as I got older and those dreams started to fade. I wasn't born with any physical gifts that would help me become a great basketball player. I was of average height, average speed, and below average jumping ability. None of this was my fault. It was genetics. I was a victim.

I worked harder and had better basketball skills than some of the players who were naturally taller, faster, and better jumpers than I was, but I still got less playing time. It didn't seem fair. If I was 6'4" and had the speed and jumping ability of Michael Jordan I could be a superstar too. I was a victim.

I remember getting really upset sitting on the bench while players who could not dribble, pass, or shoot as well as I could were starting in front of me. I spent quite a bit of time wallowing in self-pity. Part of that felt good. I had something to blame for my shortcomings other than myself. I didn't need to practice for hours every day to get better. It was my DNA's fault, and the coach's fault. Practice couldn't change that.

After a while, I started to realize I had a choice to make. I could continue to blame my physical characteristics for my lack of playing time, or I could put in the extra work to improve the areas I had control over.

I spent countless hours working on my dribbling, shooting, and passing skills. I joined the cross-country team to improve my stamina. Coach had mentioned he appreciated my efforts on defense so I worked harder than ever on my defensive skills. Through weightlifting, speed and jumping exercises I was able to slightly improve my quickness and leaping abilities.

I wasn't fooling myself. I knew there were real limitations from my physical makeup. I was not about to become LeBron James or Kobe Bryant. I never became a basketball superstar, but all my hard work did improve my playing time and my enjoyment of the game. When I went off to college, I continued to have a blast playing in the intramural leagues. I was no longer a victim, I was a victor.

Can you think of a time where you let yourself play the victim? Were you able to shake yourself out of that mindset and move in a more positive direction? How did you do it? Is this something that's stalling your progress on the journey to where you want to be?

Self-Sabotage

When things aren't going well for us it's easy to play the victim:

Didn't get the job? The boss must be racist.

Divorced three times? Your parents were bad role models.

Lost your job because you're a crack head? It's not your fault. You're an addict.

Didn't make the sale? The customer hates fat people.

Caught speeding doing 135 mph, stealing credit cards and charging hundreds of dollars to other people's bill? NASCAR made me do it. Wait …what?

Yup, as reported by *The City Paper* out of Nashville, TN:

> An inmate in federal prison has filed a $23 million lawsuit claiming NASCAR is responsible for his laundry list of criminal activity, from speeding to credit card fraud.
>
> Jonathan Lee Riches filed suit in U.S. District Court in Richmond, Va., stating that watching races "influenced him to speed … doing 135 mph and getting tickets."
>
> And that's not all. He said his NASCAR addiction caused him to use "illegally obtained credit cards to attend races," and once there, he used more stolen credit cards to purchase products hawked by race drivers.
>
> "I used (Kyle) Petty's Discover Card to buy Mark Martin Viagra," states the tardy complaint. (Viagra no longer sponsors Martin's car.)
>
> Riches said he bought race tickets using credit cards that he admitted were fraudulent, "but the defendants insisted they did not care and encouraged me to buy Budweiser beer and funnel cake with more stolen funds."
>
> He concludes by claiming that Jeff Gordon's Dupont-sponsored car "poisoned me with Dupont chemicals. I pray this court will grant my motions for relief. I don't want to die in prison."

OK, Greg, that's a ridiculous case. I'm not that bad. I have *real* reasons to feel like a victim.

I'm not even arguing that with you. My point again is, how is that belief getting you closer to the life you want? If it isn't, then why continue to be a victim?

You get to choose. Will you choose to be a victim? Will you choose to allow circumstances or someone to have power over you and stop you from living the extraordinary life you were created to lead?

Learned Helplessness

Excuses never help you with your real problems. They are actually a form of self-sabotage. Victim thoughts help you create a feeling of "learned helplessness." If you took Psychology 101 you have heard that phrase. The original experiment set up a situation where animals were given an electric jolt and there was nothing they could do to stop it. Then the experiment was changed so the animals *could* stop the shocks. However, since the animals had been taught that they had no ability to stop the pain, even when they were given the control to avoid the shocks they didn't. They were victims, so they didn't even try.

They had learned that they were helpless, so they gave up. Further research showed that humans could also fall victim to the mindset and behavior of learned helplessness.

You have probably met someone who lives their life as if they are helpless. They will tell you that nothing ever turns out right for them. They are like Eeyore from *Winnie the Pooh*. Or Glum, from *The Adventures of Gulliver* cartoon series on *The Banana Splits and Friends Show*. Remember that show? Remember the theme song? Tra La La, Tra La La La. Tra La La La La La La La. (Sorry, I loved that song as a kid.) Glum was one of four Lilliputians who were always trying to get Gulliver out of trouble. And every time the Lilliputians would come up with a plan to rescue Gulliver, Glum would say, "It'll never work," or "They're going to catch us for sure," or some other optimistic, helpful phrase.

This type of thinking stops you from doing what is necessary to succeed. It stops you from even trying to come up with a plan to turn things around. What's the point? You're a victim. Someone has done you wrong. You need to be rescued. This isn't your fault, so why should you be expected to make things better? You even start believing that this is how life will always be for you. You will always lose. People will always take advantage of you. The more you think this way, the more these things actually happen to you. They become self-fulfilling prophecies.

Self-pity is the most instructive of the non-pharmaceutical narcotics; it is addictive, gives momentary pleasure and separates the victim from reality.

–John W. Gardner, secretary of health, education, and welfare under President Lyndon Johnson

It's Not Them, It's You

At one point in my junior basketball season, my team wasn't doing very well. During a timeout one of the players said to my coach, "These plays aren't working." My coach said, "You're right. They don't work with *you. You're* out." Coach then put another player in and said, "Now execute the plays the way we practiced them." Guess what? All of a sudden those same plays started to work. The first player saw himself as a victim of a bad game plan. It wasn't his fault the team was playing poorly, it was the bad plays. The second player, and the rest of the team, believed that if they executed those plays properly they would work. They were right. It goes back to the idea of whether you believe you can or believe you can't, you are right.

Rewards of Victimhood

Some people seem to want to become victims. I counseled some people like this when I worked in the mental health field. At first blush, it didn't make much sense. Why would you want to be a victim when so many bad things are associated with it? It is easier to comprehend when you see how we reward victims. Victims are celebrated as heroes in books, movies, and television. There appear to be lots of good reasons to want to be a victim. Here's just a short, incomplete list of them.

- You are not expected to do much of anything, certainly not work hard and succeed.
- You have no responsibility for what happened to you.

- You have a *right* to be depressed and angry.
- You are *entitled* to a bottomless pit of sympathy.
- You have a *right* to be rescued.
- You may win millions of dollars in a lawsuit.
- You may accuse your boss of discrimination, get your old job back with back pay or with a promotion.
- No one can question you or they are "blaming the victim."

Playing the "Don't Blame the Victim" Card

The idea of not blaming the victim makes perfect sense. Much of the idea came from the way rape victims were treated in court. Quite often, descriptions of the victim were used to take the responsibility away from the criminal. Let's be clear: It is *never* the victim's fault that she or he is raped. The way she was dressed, or how drunk she was, or what neighborhood she was in, or how late she was walking home alone did not force someone to rape her. She, or he, is the victim. It's the rapist's fault.

Having said all that, the idea of not blaming the victim has turned into never questioning the victim's role in the situation. We are now told that we can't even talk about bad choices a victim may have made, because that's blaming the victim. Unfortunately, that also means the victim had zero *control* over what happened to her. This really makes her a double victim. It's also just not true.

It is not Desiree Washington's fault that Mike Tyson raped her. However, knowing the history of "Iron Mike" with women, it's just plain stupid to go up to Mike Tyson's hotel room, alone, at 3 a.m. Both of those things can be true at the same time. Plus, it gives the victim some control over future, similar situations. Isn't that a *good* thing?

If you are mugged while walking home from a bar it is not your fault. However, if you were so drunk you could barely walk and you were in a crime-ridden area of town, then you have some responsibility for putting yourself in that ridiculous situation. Understanding what role your behavior can play in controlling a situation where you might become a victim is actually extremely empowering and not "blaming the victim."

Thankfully, most of us will never have to deal with anything as painful and traumatic as rape, but we will have many opportunities to allow ourselves to become victims. Figuring out who is to blame in a situation may have its place, but it does not solve the problem. An old expression puts it well, "Fix the problem, not the blame."

What If I'm a *Real* Victim?

The greatest griefs are those we cause ourselves.

–Sophocles, Greek playwright

You might be thinking to yourself right now, "Greg is a moron. Some people really are victims. Sometimes it's really not their fault." And you know what? You're right (except for that moron part). Sometimes you are a real victim of racism, or fatism, or sexism, or whatever other -ism you can come up with. Maybe you are a victim of a disease, crime, or natural disaster.

But even if you are a true victim, how is being a victim going to help you make your life better? It won't. It *can't*. So it's up to you to say, "No matter what has happened to me in my past I am not going to let that become my future. I am not going to let anyone or anything have the power to ruin my life."

That doesn't mean all the pain and depression will go away overnight. But realizing that maintaining your victim status will do nothing to help you overcome your current situation is absolutely necessary to getting you back on the path to success.

"I'm Not a Victim"

This above all, to refuse to be a victim.

–Margaret Atwood, poet and novelist

Retired United States Army Staff Sergeant Travis Mills served three tours in Afghanistan before a roadside bomb hit him. He thought it was over. He even told the medic to leave him alone because he thought he had no chance to live. He lost all four limbs that day. What motivated him to stay alive were his wife and infant daughter back home.

When he got to Walter Reed Medical Center he was feeling pretty bad about his future. Travis told me what kick-started his recovery was when another quadruple amputee soldier, Todd Nicely, came into his room and said, "You're going to get through this." That was the beginning of a long, painful process.

Travis now snowboards, bikes, and even skydives. He created a nonprofit foundation to help other wounded warriors get back on their feet. He is a motivational speaker and he tours with a documentary about his recovery.

On my radio show he said, "I'm not a victim. Everybody has problems." I couldn't believe what a great attitude he had. Everybody has problems? Yes, but most of us let bad cell phone coverage ruin our day. If we get the wrong order at the drive-through we may be in a funk for hours. Travis is a *quadruple* amputee and he's not complaining. Kind of puts it all in perspective doesn't it?

Travis told me that his prosthetics are so great that there's nothing he can't do now. He's enjoying life with his wife and child. His motto is: "Never give up. Never quit." He is definitely not a victim.

Your Response and Attitude Can Change You from a Victim to a Victor

You can't be a victim and heal.

–A. J. Langer, actress

The way you respond to being victimized can determine whether you recover and move forward with your life or stay locked in a cycle of blame, resentment, and depression. You can see this in the way people responded to the devastating tornado that hit Greensburg, Kansas, in 2007.

A powerful F5 tornado destroyed the town of 1,500 people. The storm hit just before 10 o'clock at night. Thankfully, the residents had some warning and only eight people lost their lives. Almost every building and tree was knocked down by the tornado. Yet, by morning, almost every road had been cleared of debris. Local government agencies helped some. Volunteer fire departments arrived almost as soon as the storm ended. But most of the clearing of the roads was done by ordinary citizens of Greensburg and nearby towns. They grabbed their chainsaws, jumped in their pickup trucks, and started working to help their neighbors and friends. They didn't wait for someone else to save them.

They were real victims of a natural disaster, but they didn't act like it. They couldn't change the fact that the tornado had destroyed their town, but they knew they were in control of what happened after the storm. They knew they had the power to control what happened *next.* They knew they could *choose* to be victims or to become victors.

Dennis Boyles wrote about this type of attitude for *National Review Online* as he covered the aftermath of the tornado.

> Not long ago, while I was working on my book about the Midwest, I met a woman in her 80s in McCook, Nebraska, who told me about how she and her family had escaped the Republican River flood of 1935. That was the flood that hit in the middle of the Dust Bowl, dropped ten years' worth of water in a few hours, and turned the nearly dry riverbed into a

> sea nearly four miles wide. She and her mother and father had survived by running to a nearby farm situated on the only hill around. When the water reached the farmhouse, they ran for the barn. When it reached the barn, they ran for the machine shed. When it reached the machine shed, the climbed into the rafters. They won by inches. When they finally climbed down, they were like the people in Greensburg: Alone, with nothing, on a big, flat, hostile plain. I asked her what the government did to help them out. She looked at me like I was nuts. "The government? We never even thought of that. We just went back to work."

We just went back to work. That's the attitude we need whenever we feel like a victim. It's not easy, but it gets amazing results.

You cannot be a victim and live out your Passionate Purpose. You must understand that *you*, not your parents, society, your government, or anyone else, *you* have the power to determine what your future will be. It doesn't matter if your victimhood is real or phony. Tune out the voices in your head that are blaming, complaining, and whining about your lot in life. Reframe everything in your past in the most positive way you can. Even the worst circumstances can teach us something. That doesn't mean that everything that has happened to you was good. It means you are choosing to use it for your good in the future. You are choosing to make everything in your past part of what is making you stronger and better. That's empowering.

Get it deep in your soul. Until you give up blaming other people or circumstances for your failures and change your mindset from victim to victor, you will never truly succeed.

Equal Opportunity Does Not Mean Equal Outcomes

> *To every disadvantage there is a corresponding advantage.*
>
> –W. Clement Stone, author, businessman, philanthropist

America prides itself on the idea of equal opportunity. That used to mean that if you work hard enough, you can live out your dreams. Over time, though, the idea of equal opportunity has morphed into a demand of a "right" to equal outcomes. After all, that's the only way for everyone to get their "fair share." But there will never be equal outcomes, not because the system is "unfair," but because we have unequal inputs.

I readily agree that it's not "fair" that everyone doesn't start from the same point in this world. Some people have it harder than others. But all of us have *something* we must overcome in order to achieve the outcome we desire. And all of us are born with *something* that makes us unique and *something* that will help us succeed. The key is deciding not to be a victim and to fully exploit all the opportunity we have in this country.

Those who succeed are the ones who do not let their disadvantages define them. They're the ones who don't waste their time complaining about the hand life dealt them. They understand that living life as a victim limits your true potential and comes with strings attached that curtail your freedom.

Sometimes you can even use what some consider your shortcomings to your advantage.

A young boy was missing his left arm after a horrible automobile accident. After dealing with some depression, a friend of his got him to start studying judo. Some of the other kids asked him how he was going to do all the moves with only one arm. The boy had no good answer.

He found a judo school run by an old Japanese master who agreed to take him on, even with his handicap.

The boy began lessons with the elderly sensei and was doing well. However, he didn't understand why the master taught him only one judo move. For months the boy practiced his one throwing technique over and over.

"Sensei," the boy finally said, "Shouldn't I be learning more moves?"

"I know I have only taught you one technique, but this is the only move you need to know," the master replied.

Not quite understanding, but putting his faith in his teacher, the boy kept training.

Several months later, the sensei took the boy to his first tournament. Surprising himself, the boy easily won his first two matches. The third match proved to be more difficult, but after some time, his opponent became impatient and over extended his balance. The boy deftly used his one move to win the match. Still amazed by his success, the boy was now in the finals.

This time, his opponent was bigger, stronger, and more experienced. For a while, the boy appeared to be in real trouble. Concerned that the boy might get hurt, the referee called a time-out. He was about to stop the match when the sensei intervened.

"No," the sensei insisted, "Let him continue."

Soon after the match resumed, his opponent made a critical mistake; He dropped his guard. Instantly, the boy used his move to throw and pin his opponent. The boy not only won the match, but he won the tournament. He was the champion!

On the way home, the boy asked, "Sensei, how did I win the tournament with only one move?"

"You won for two reasons," the teacher answered. "First, you've almost mastered one of the most difficult throws in all of judo. And second, the only known defense for that move is for your opponent to grab your left arm."

"The One-Armed Judoka" –Author unkown

Circumstances, event, tragedies, and what people have done to you do not have the power to make you a victim unless you give them that power. You get to decide. Your responses, your attitude, and the way you frame things in your mind can help or hurt you. What will you choose?

Techniques from the Masters

- When you see yourself as a victim you are helpless, hopeless, depressed, self-pitying, blaming, negative, and unlovable.
- Your victimhood can be real or imagined, but no matter what bad hand life has dealt you, the beginning of your way out is knowing and believing that you control what happens to you from this point forward.
- Playing the victim gives you short-term rewards, but long-term pain. Focus on how the pain will continue if you don't change and how you can end that pain and reach your goals by doing the work to stop being a victim.
- Reframe everything in your past in the most positive way you can.
- Choose to make everything in your past part of what is making you stronger and better. That's empowering.

Commitment

How to Stay Committed to Your Purpose and Your Why

Man is only great when he acts from passion.

–Benjamin Disraeli, novelist and former prime minister of the United Kingdom

There is a reason we started by finding your Passionate Purpose. The best way to overcome all obstacles in your journey is to have a great Passionate Purpose for what you are doing. If your only purpose is to make money, you probably won't make it. This whole journey is fueled by your why. Why are you really doing this? If the "why" is great enough, you will get through any "how" or "what." Every time you hit a wall, refocus on your why.

Why? For me, it isn't about becoming a billionaire (although I do have substantial income goals). It isn't about getting so busy that I'm working 60 to 80 hours a week. It's not about what my parents, peers, or anyone else thinks I should be doing. It's about enjoying my life's work—enjoying my Passionate Purpose.

As long as I'm doing that, I'm living the extraordinary life I was created to live. I am *free*. Free to do what I want, live where I want, be with whom I want, give and share what I want, and travel where I want. Freedom from the ordinary life.

More Than One Why

When I really think about it, I have more than one why for pursuing my Passionate Purpose. I want to do what I believe I was created to do, not just get by. I want to inspire and motivate other people to do the same. I want to help other people throw off the chains keeping them in a mediocre life. I also want to help other people get what they want so I can get everything I want. I want *freedom.*

My friend Dick Bott, founder of Bott Radio says, "Financial freedom is the ability to be creative without financial worry. If worry and fear are present, the wolf is at the door. Your creativity dries up." That resonates with me. Don't we all want to do what energizes us for our work as well as for our play? It sure beats working 40-60 hours a week to pay the bills so you can try to get your soul back every weekend.

What is it for you? What's your *ultimate* why? It's OK to have more than one, but under it all there is one *special* why. Find it. Keep it front and center in your mind as you put forth all the work necessary to turn your dreams into reality.

My ultimate *financial* goal is to use my Passionate Purpose to bring in enough active and passive income so I can maintain the lifestyle I desire while "working" as much, or as little, as I want to.

At that point you will have all the time you want to be with your family and friends. You'll have time to help others through your church and charities.

Freedom

When you and I reach that point, our time will be our own. You've heard the expression "Time is money." That's not true. Time is more valuable than money. You can make more money. You can't make more time. So far, no one can. Time is freedom. And that's my ultimate why. You will have time to travel, learn a foreign language, play an instrument, or anything you've ever wanted to do.

For … the … rest … of … your … *life.*

> *Dost thou love life? Then do not squander time, for that's the stuff life is made of.*
>
> –Benjamin Franklin, Founding Father, printer, writer, scientist, inventor, statesman, civic leader, and diplomat.

If you are doing this right and really find your true calling you will probably never want to fully retire. You enjoy your work, so why quit? You can decide how much or how little you want to do each day that most people would call "work." Wouldn't that be amazing?

So I spend a little time every day imagining and visualizing what that's going to be like. Some people call this daydreaming. If that's all I did every day I would agree. But the way I do it, it's motivational planning, it's emotional adrenaline, it's Passionate Purpose fuel, and it's preparation for the future. I try to imagine what my life will look, feel, sound, taste, and smell like. I make it as real as I can in my mind and I hold onto it for a little while. I'm doing what I love, serving others, providing a great life for my family, and creating more time for all the things on my bucket list. It's a great feeling and it helps remind me that all the hard work is worth it.

That's part of my practice to keep myself in a positive mindset. Each of us has a tremendous ability to create our own attitude no matter what situation we are in. I'm sure you've noticed in your life how much your outlook can affect your day.

But then I do something every day to get me where I'm going. I actually do something. *Action* is necessary to move forward and pursue your Passionate Purpose. It doesn't just happen by magic. You need to do something every day and build on what you did yesterday. The way to get the future you want is to do something today and then do something again tomorrow. Keep doing that and before you know it all your little efforts in the present have added up to a great life in the future.

Never Give Up

Have you ever given up at something? I have. It made me feel lousy. It made me feel like a failure, like someone who would never do anything great. It made it easier to quit the next time. I credit one of my coaches for shaking me out of that funk. He pushed me harder physically and mentally than I had ever been pushed before. When I was tired, he wouldn't let me quit. When I thought I wasn't being treated fairly, he pushed me to find a way to make things better. When I thought I couldn't go one more step, he encouraged me to go ten more. After a while I started to realize that the only way you can truly fail is to give up. That sounds simple and corny, but it's true. If you never give up, you can't fail. Get that in your head. Write it down. Hang it on your bathroom mirror. Read it when you get up in the morning and before you go to bed at night.

Never give up.

Winston Churchill was invited to give the commencement address at Oxford and used the theme "Never Give Up" as the thrust of his speech. In fact, he believed so strongly in how important it was to never give up that he simply stood up, said, "Never give in," and sat back down. Great story, bro, but according to the Churchill Centre it isn't true.

The real story is just as good if not better. Churchill gave a speech when he returned to his alma mater, Harrow School, in 1941. He did keep it short and to the point.

> *This is the lesson: never give in, never give in, never, never, never, never—in nothing, great or small, large or petty—never give in except to convictions of honour and good sense. Never yield to force; never yield to the apparently overwhelming might of the enemy.*
>
> –Winston Churchill, Harrow School, 1941.

Walter loved to draw and sketch. He worked hard at it and developed great skill. He was able to use these skills and his aptitude for photography on his high school newspaper. He eventually got a job at *The Kansas City Star*, but was quickly fired for what his boss said was a "lack of creativity."

Walter then put his drawing skills to work with a company making short films. He really enjoyed that, learned a lot, and decided to start out on his own. He created a series of shorts but his company floundered and went bankrupt.

Walt experienced failure after failure. Some would-be employers even questioned his "artistic integrity." Could it be that drawing, art, and making movies wasn't what Walter was really supposed to do? Maybe he should quit what so many people told him was just silly cartoons and think about getting a real job.

No. This was what he had always wanted to do. He packed up and moved west to Los Angeles. Through much persistence and hard work, the movie industry decided he could be of use to them after all.

Walt Disney went on to create the first sound-synchronized cartoon. He made the first feature-length animated film, *Snow White and the Seven Dwarfs*. He held the patent on Technicolor and used it to greatly improve his animation.

His success led him to achieve another one of his dreams, creating the first permanent, family-friendly, clean amusement park in the United States. He planned it out for seven years. It wasn't easy to get funding or get approval from the city of Anaheim. At first the city council rejected the idea because they were worried about Disneyland bringing in the wrong type of crowd. But Walter never quit.

When he was looking for funding for his first big cartoon, 300 bankers rejected him. They thought his idea of a cartoon about a mouse was ridiculous. How interesting that Mickey Mouse ended up starting it all for Walt.

His driving will to keep moving forward and never give up led him to build more amusement parks, water parks, and hotel resorts. It even led his company to buy ABC, which, at the time, owned *The Kansas City Star*.

Yup, the newspaper that fired him for "lack of creativity" all those years ago.

> *All our dreams can come true, if we have the courage to pursue them.*
>
> –Walt Disney, cartoonist, filmmaker, visionary, and developer

Sometimes It's OK to Quit

Greg, you're freaking me out again. Didn't you just tell me to never give up? Now you're telling me it's OK to quit? Are you off your meds?

I understand the confusion. But there's a big difference between giving up and deciding to quit something. If you stop working towards what you know is your Passionate Purpose because it's too hard, or someone talked you out of it, or you got sidetracked on unimportant things, or you had to watch the Simpsons marathon on FX, that's giving up. That's what I hope you won't do.

If, however, you are trying out new things to see what fits on you, it's perfectly OK to stop doing something you find out you truly don't enjoy. How will you know what you really like if you don't try it? I don't want you to feel like once you try something new you can never quit or you're a failure.

What if you discover it wasn't really your Passionate Purpose after all? What if you realize you're trying to live out the dream your parents have for your life, or you're trying to please someone else? Wouldn't it be crazy to keep pursuing someone else's goals?

How do you know the difference between giving up and quitting? Here's what I do and what I make my children do. If you want to try something new, like a sport, an instrument, dance lessons, or a new job, determine a set amount of time that you are going to continue trying it no matter what. A rule of thumb is six months to a year. If you decide you don't like it at the end of your trial period, you can quit without being a "quitter." You aren't quitting because you can't stick with something. You did stick with it. You did what you set out to do. You learned it wasn't a good fit for you and now you're moving on to something else.

If it is a good fit for you, keep doing it! You're on your way.

Techniques from the Masters:

- Focus on your “why” and make it as real and strong as possible. The stronger your “why” the easier it will be to get you through your “hows” and “whats.”
- Making money is a good thing. However, if that is your only “why” you probably won’t make it.
- Have fun and enjoy the process.
- Never give up on your Passionate Purpose. Quite often the only difference between failure and immense success is one gave up and one didn’t.
- Sometimes it’s OK to quit. It’s not the same as giving up. Try new things and new ways. Give yourself a length of time to stick with it. If it’s working and you like it, keep going. Otherwise, try something else.
- Spend time every day visualizing your life with your ultimate goal achieved. Create the feeling of what it would be like if that life already existed for you. Imagine what it would look, feel, sound, smell, and taste like. Make it as real as possible in your mind and body.
- Take action every day that supports your “why” and leads you to your goals.

A Lifelong Process

How to Enjoy Pursuing Your
Passionate Purpose for the Rest of Your Life

Keep Learning and Growing

I guess it comes down to a simple choice, really. Get busy living or get busy dying.

–The character Andy from *The Shawshank Redemption*

Following your Passionate Purpose doesn't mean you only do one thing to earn a living. What happens if that one thing changes so much you can't or don't want to do it anymore? What happens to you and your family then?

The days of getting a good job and working there until you retire are over. The global economy is so dynamic now; it's difficult to predict what is going to happen in the future. The only thing we know for sure is there will be change. We need to ***start*** by figuring out what we want and why. Then, follow our lifelong process of pursuing our Passionate Purpose. We will develop many different ways and reasons to do this. It's smart and rewarding to develop multiple streams of income from what you enjoy doing.

I can earn money while helping people and pursuing my Passionate Purpose by writing books, eBooks, audiobooks, giving speeches, creating seminars and DVD courses. I'm still cultivating other ideas off my Passionate Purpose as well. My plans include writing a new book every year.

I'm continually learning how to:

- Find new ways to follow my Passionate Purpose
- Fully enjoy my dream occupation
- Master new skills in my field
- Develop new income sources with what I love to do
- Grow spiritually
- Improve my marriage
- Connect with my children
- Become fluent in Spanish
- Play guitar
- Improve my physical health
- Read and understand financial statements
- Buy and sell houses, apartments, and commercial properties
- Negotiate deals
- Trade and invest in the markets

I do all this to be prepared for my future, to take care of my family, and to get where I want to go. Most of this is fun stuff that I actually enjoy doing. Don't get me wrong, everything isn't rainbows and unicorns, but I refuse to work my whole life doing what I hate.

This is also the smart way to go in the so-called New Economy. The bottom line is you never know what's coming. I found this out the hard way.

I thought I had arrived. Everything was going according to plan. I had achieved my dream of becoming a nationally syndicated talk radio host. I was on more than 60 radio stations nationwide. I had a safe two-year contract with my syndicator. Everyone told me they loved my show. They told me I was "the future host" for the company. Then the recession hit, the company lost tons of advertising revenue, and I was informed they couldn't afford to renew my contract. No one had lied to me or treated me poorly. They still loved my show, but the economics didn't work anymore. Circumstances had changed.

Thankfully, I was already pursuing my Passionate Purpose and had options. My wife and I had put enough money away in our emergency fund to last eight months. I was working on a documentary on wasteful government spending, beginning to write this book, and working on investing more in real estate. Unfortunately, I didn't have all these sources of income up and running before I lost my job.

Because I was already thinking this way, I was able to find work as a guest radio host for nationally syndicated talkers when they were out on vacation, and for talk shows all around the country. I filled in as the interim music leader at my church, and got my real estate license. All that, and my wife's job as an elementary school teacher kept us going until I landed my next full-time gig as a radio talk show host in Kansas City.

My situation absolutely confirmed for me the need for all Americans to change their mindset on what the American dream is and how to get it.

You Have More Time Than You Think

Yes, this work takes time and you're busy. But everyone gets the same amount of time every day, yet some seem to get more done in the same 24 hours. How? The place to start is to figure out how you currently spend your time. And that is the precise way to talk about time. We do *spend* it. We all have a limited amount of time on this planet hurtling through space. We are all *spending* it doing something every minute of every day. Are you spending it wisely for what you want to become and do? Let's find out.

Keep a log of how you spend your leisure time for one full week. Write down everything. Sleeping, getting ready for work, commute time, work time, lunch, dinner, family time, television, email, web surfing, social media, golf, workouts, going out with friends, church, phone calls, etc. I know it can be tiresome to do this, but we're only doing it for one week to see where your time goes. I bet you will be shocked at what you are spending something *more* valuable than money on.

You will be surprised how much you can get done just by turning off the television. Americans watch an average of four hours of TV *a day*. All television isn't bad and we all need a total couch potato break every now and then. But if you plan out exactly what you want to watch at the beginning of the week and only turn on the TV for those shows, you could free up to 20 hours each week to devote to your Passionate Purpose.

Maybe TV isn't where you waste your time. How about the Internet? I know it sucks me in. I plan to just answer a few emails and the next thing I know, I'm watching a funny clip from *Britain's Got Talent*, or a funny YouTube clip a friend sent me, and an hour of my life is gone. Throw in Twitter, email, Facebook, and Pinterest and you could lose another hour in the blink of an eye.

Don't let technology steal your life from you. Plan your time. Stay focused. When you need to unwind, actively choose the best way for you to do that. Don't default into channel surfing or playing on the computer because it's the easiest thing to do. Live *purposefully.*

We all need leisure time, but plan it out purposefully. What do you love to do to relax? Plan for it in your daily and weekly calendar. Live intentionally. Don't allow your limited downtime to be eaten up by default activities you really don't care about, like watching a repeat of *Tic-Tac-Dough* on the Game Show Network. I watched that once and I could actually feel my life force slipping away. Don't give in to the dark side! Live intentionally.

A Gift of an Extra Hour a Day

You're busy. You work full time. You work around the house. You have a family that needs your time, care, and attention. If you're like me, you are wiped out by the end of the night when everyone is finally put to bed. When do you have the time and energy to pursue your Passionate Purpose?

What would you say if I could give you an extra hour every day? Sound good?

Here's how you get it: Wake up one hour early.

What?! I don't get enough sleep as it is. When did you start smoking meth, Greg? Did you miss that big discussion we had about how busy I am?

Hey, I understand. You're right. (Except for that part about me smoking meth. I kind of want to keep my teeth and not look like someone raised by wolves on the Appalachian Trail in the 1930s.) Sleep is very important. So instead of popping on the TV, how about getting to bed early so you're rested enough to get up earlier?

But I'm not a morning person!

I'm not either. But you know what? I've come to love getting up before everyone else in the house does. (Now, my life is a little different. I do a morning radio show and I rise at 2:50 a.m. to get ready. But even on the weekends I get up before the family.) The morning is quiet. No one bothers you. No one is calling or emailing you. No one is demanding you do something for them right *now*. It can be a great start to your day. You can get your coffee or tea, pray or meditate, and get prepared for the day. Then you can get an hour in on your new Passionate Purpose project. You are going to feel awesome when you do this (not the waking up part, but the getting stuff done for *you* part).

Andy Traub has written a great book on how to get up early. He helps you get this new habit started with uplifting daily messages, support groups, and apps. Check it out at http://www.earlytorisebook.com/

Spend Time in Your Mobile University

Be not afraid of growing slowly; be afraid only of standing still.

–Chinese Proverb

The average commute time in America is around 24 minutes each way. Instead of looking at this as wasted time, why not get an hour of studying in every day on your car stereo, iPod, or smart phone? I download courses on personal development, motivation, foreign languages, history, real estate, and more. You can find all kinds of great programs on CD for free at your local library. I bet you can find things that will help you improve your skills to pursue your Passionate Purpose. It sure beats the road rage I used to get sitting in traffic. You can do the same thing while you work out. I even listen to my Spanish language tapes while I lift weights and jog. OK, I almost never jog. I … hate … running. I do enjoy lifting weights, walking, playing basketball, surfing, and jumping rope. (I also like pina coladas and getting caught in the rain. But I'm already taken, ladies! Sorry.)

Estimates are that we spend 45 to 62 minutes waiting in lines *every day.* I got so tired of it that I started carrying a book wherever I went. Now when I'm stuck in line at the post office or the grocery store I don't get annoyed, I just start reading my book. In addition to increasing my study time, it makes for a much more pleasant day. Sometimes I meditate or say my prayers. That sets me up for a much more positive attitude by the time I get to the front of the line. Then I try to be super nice to the cashier to brighten her day. It usually works and then both of us feel better. I know this sounds a little corny, but I love corny. It brings me joy. Why not try it and see what it does for you?

Your motivation will rise and fall throughout your days, months, and years. It happens to everyone. The key is to figure out how to stoke your fire and keep yourself motivated.

Focus on your why. Do what you love. Keep learning new things and developing new skills. Stay focused on your most important goals. Revel in the joy that comes from pursuing your Passionate Purpose and living the life you've always dreamed of. Attend seminars from people you respect in your field. Keep growing and developing yourself every way you can.

Sometimes we get so caught up in achieving our goals that we miss out on what's happening to us along the way. Don't let that happen. Enjoy all that the process will bring you. As you pursue your Passionate Purpose you will improve and become more than you used to be. You will develop new skills, gain experience, and gather new information. You will grow into a better person.

It's impossible to truly achieve your goals without improving yourself. Remember to enjoy achieving your goals and enjoying the process you went through to achieve them. It's your life, after all. Shouldn't you enjoy it?

Techniques from the Masters:

- As you follow your Passionate Purpose create multiple streams of income from what you enjoy doing.
- *Spend* your limited time on this planet wisely.
- For one week keep a log of how you spend every minute of each day. Purposefully decide what is worth doing and what you should stop doing.
- Go to bed on time so you can wake up one hour early. You will be amazed by what you will accomplish during this gift of personal alone time. It will greatly benefit your soul as well.
- Plan your leisure time, not just your work time. Live intentionally.
- Make a commitment to yourself to constantly grow and develop in every way you can.
- Turn your car into Mobile University. Use your commuting and driving time to listen to books, upgrade your skills, learn a new language, and more.

Motivation

How to Stay Motivated and Make Lasting Change

OK, Greg, I've been reading this book and using the techniques. I'm fired up like a BBQ grill on Memorial Day. I'm feeling as high as Willie Nelson at a NORML convention. But I've gotten excited about changing my life before and the feeling wore off. How do I stay motivated? How do I change my behavior, long term, to get what I want?

Great question. Your motivation will go up and down. No one stays super motivated all the time. You're not happy all the time, or sad all the time. You don't even feel like going to the beach or watching a movie all the time. So why should you feel motivated all the time? It's not realistic.

We've talked about this before, but it's worth repeating. People who say getting motivated and working on improving yourself are a waste of time because it wears off need to really think that through. Doesn't everything wear off if you don't keep up with it?

I play the guitar and I used to play the trumpet. When I play in a band I make sure I tune my instrument before we begin. Guess what? The instruments don't *stay* in tune. I re-tune them every other song or so. If I'm playing my guitar with my band at an outside gig where it's exceptionally hot or cold, I may re-tune after *every* song.

I take a shower every day. I eat three times a day. I lift weights three times a week. I practice my guitar every day. I listen to my Spanish tapes every day on the way to work.

Why do I have to do these things every day? If I do them once, shouldn't that be enough?

That sounds crazy doesn't it?

Imagine a doctor who says, "Well, I've graduated med school and passed my boards, now I'll never need to study anything else or do anymore training for the rest of my career." Would you want to go to that doctor?

> *Somewhere in the world is the world's worst doctor. And what's truly terrifying is that someone has an appointment with him tomorrow morning.*
>
> –George Carlin, comedian, actor

Everything wears off if we don't work to improve our skills. What we need to do is build in ways to boost our motivation when it starts to lag. We need a way to create new habits of behavior so that what you need to do to succeed becomes as automatic as tying your shoes or brushing your teeth.

Lock In Your New Thoughts and Behaviors

We've created some great ways to build our motivation:

- You've discovered your Passionate Purpose.
- You've written down your goals.
- You have yearly, monthly, weekly, and even daily plans to reach those goals.
- You have an "accountability partner" you talk with every week so that you stay on track.
- You are taking action every day on your Passionate Purpose.
- You're using the new skills and behaviors you've learned in this book to create your new life.

Now it's time to lock in your new thoughts and behaviors. How?

Who am I?

I am your constant companion.

I am your greatest helper or your heaviest burden.

I will push you onward or drag you down to failure.

I am completely at your command.

Half the things you do, you might just as well turn over to me and I will be able to do them quickly and correctly.

I am easily managed, you must merely be firm with me.

Show me exactly how you want something done, and after a few lessons I will do it automatically.

I am the servant of all great men, and alas, of all failures as well.

Those who are great, I have made them great.

Those who are failures, I have made failures.

I am not a machine though I work with the precision of a machine, plus the intelligence of man.

You may run me for profit, or run me for ruin;

It makes no difference to me.

Take me, train me, be firm with me,
and I will put the world at your feet.

Be easy with me and I will destroy you.

Who am I?

I am Habit!

–Anonymous

Most of what we do each day is actually habitual. Think about it. You wake up at the same time. You have the same ritual on how and when you shower, shave, put on your clothes, get your coffee, eat or don't eat breakfast. You take the same route to work. You do the same things every day as soon as you get to work. You have habits on how you do the routine parts of your job. You have a habitual routine at night before you go to sleep. We are creatures of habit.

Habits can work for us or against us. We can create and continue bad habits that take us away from where we want to go, or we can create and maintain positive habits that lead to a success that's almost automatic. Which one sounds good to you? (No, that's not a trick question.)

In *The Power of Habit* by Charles Duhigg, the habit loop is explained. It goes like this: Cue – Routine – Reward – Repeat.

First, there is a cue, or a trigger. It could be a smell, a time of day, a friend, a song, an emotional state, etc. This sets you up for your habitual behavior. You don't even consciously think about making the decision to act any more. It's automatic.

The behavior is your routine. This could be eating a sweet, goofing off on your Facebook page, going for a run, biting your fingernails, or smoking a cigarette.

The behavior leads to your reward. This is what keeps the habit going. The reward could be the taste of the sweet, or the emotional feeling you get with the taste, or the break you get from being at your desk all day, or the nicotine in the cigarette, or the connection you get with people on Facebook.

You need to find out what your real rewards are for the habits you don't like and the rewards you would like to set up for the habits you want to develop or keep.

Duhigg found a process for breaking bad habits and replacing them with beneficial ones. That last part is key. It's much easier to stop a habit you don't like when you replace it with a new habit loop.

> *The Golden Rule of Habit Change: You can't extinguish a bad habit, you can only change it.*
>
> –Charles Duhigg

This idea makes breaking bad habits much easier. You aren't really getting rid of any habits, you're changing them to habits that help you instead of ones that hurt you.

Think of it this way. When you go into a dark room, do you try to pull the dark out? No, you light a candle and create light to replace the dark. It's the same way with your bad habits. Instead of trying to get rid of the bad ones, we're going to add good ones to force the bad ones out.

The "bad" habit loop you're trying to change keeps the same cue and the same reward. All you do is change the routine. When you do this often enough and long enough, your "new" habit will become just as automatic as the old one.

Wouldn't it be great to take control of the habits that run most of our lives? Wouldn't it be great to consciously create good habits that will help take us where we want to go? We *can* do exactly that. It's not always easy, but Duhigg explains how we can do it. Pick up his book to learn more.

Once you lock in the new behaviors we've been working on into habits, it will be easier to stay motivated for the long term. But don't think it will be one smooth ride. You will have days when you don't feel like doing the work it takes to reach your goal. You will have days when you don't feel motivated enough to even get out of bed. We've all been there.

Re-motivate

Here are some ideas on how to get re-motivated when you're starting to feel down:

- Call your accountability partner.
- Reread parts of this book.

- Go on YouTube and listen to a motivational message.
- Attend a motivational seminar.
- Refresh your memory on why you're working on these goals.
- Reward yourself for the progress you've made so far.

I always come back to the "why." Why are you working this hard? Why are you doing what other people aren't willing to do? Because then you will get to do what other people aren't able to do.

Imagine you are living the life you've always wanted. You have the relationships, career, money, family, home, and lifestyle you've only dreamed about. What exactly would your life be like if that was true? Visualize it. Imagine it. What would it look, sound, smell, feel, and taste like? Really feel the feelings you will have when you are living your extraordinary life. Simmer in those feelings for five or 10 minutes.

Are you feeling motivated yet?

Give Yourself Some Grace

> *The meaning of life. The wasted years of life. The poor choices of life. God answers the mess of life with one word: grace.*
>
> –Max Lucado, Christian author, writer, and preacher

We all have so much we want to do in a day, week, or month that when we don't get it all done we start to "should" on ourselves, as Dr. Albert Ellis used to say.

"I should've said …"

"I should've done …"

"I should've been there …"

"I should've gotten more work done …"

"I should've finished my book, blog, etc. …"

Anytime we start "shoulding" on ourselves, things are going to get messy and we're going to feel bad. Before we do that, we need to ask ourselves if that's going to help. Will playing those tapes criticizing ourselves over and over in our heads lead to good feelings? Will it motivate us? Or will it just bring us down and make it less likely for us to achieve our goals?

I'm not saying ignore a time when you are having trouble getting motivated. Evaluate it objectively. Determine how to get back on track. Readjust your timeline if you need to. But give yourself some grace and then get back in the game.

Following your Passionate Purpose to achieve your goals should be enjoyable; don't let stress ruin it for you.

> *Nobody who ever gave his best regretted it.*
>
> –George Halas, owner, coach, and player in professional football

Procrastination Paralyzes

Have you ever said, "I'm done for today. I'll do it tomorrow. I'm not in the mood right now"? Unless you're super human, I'm guessing at some time in your life you've said all those things. We all get tired or down. Procrastination gets everyone from time to time. It will paralyze you and kill your dreams, if you let it.

This is where your mini-goals come in. Remember those? Remember the plan of taking action every day to get to your short, medium, and long-term goals? Remember how your future is made up of what you do in all your right nows? Well, procrastination will stop all that if you're not careful.

My wife and I had let our garage turn into a disaster area. We couldn't park either car in it. It was jammed full with junk. The idea of cleaning it out seemed overwhelming. It would take forever and it certainly wouldn't be fun. We let the garage sit like that for months.

Finally, I read about the 15-minute technique. It's simple. The idea is that you can do anything for 15 minutes. So Anne and I decided that we would clean a small area of the garage for 15 minutes every day. Once that area was clean we would move on to the next area.

As much as we hated cleaning the garage, knowing that it would be over in 15 minutes made it easy for us to jump in. We put our favorite music on, set the timer, and started working. We were both shocked at how quickly the timer went off. We were even more surprised at the progress we had made in such a short time. We kept at it every day. Most days, we would get into it and work more than the 15 minutes we had set aside. It wasn't as bad as we thought it would be once we got started. We finished that garage off way faster than we thought we would. It looked great and we felt great.

It is truly amazing the momentum you can create when you take action. What action on your goals have you taken today? Even 15 minutes will make a world of difference. Give it a try.

Techniques from the Masters

- Realize that motivation is an ongoing process like exercising or eating and not a one-time thing.
- Be aware of when your motivational level is low.
- Use the habit loop to change your bad habits into good ones.
- Get back in touch with your "why."
- Imagine what it will feel like to be living your dream life.
- Utilize the methods in this chapter to re-motivate.
- Give yourself some grace.
- Use the 15-minute technique.

Conclusion:

It's Time to Go

Earlier we talked about the scene in the movie *Knight and Day* where the two characters discussed how dangerous the word "someday" can be. Often it's just code for "never."

At the very end of the film, June and Roy are in her restored GTO on a beach in Mexico. June has rescued Roy from the bad guys and found the courage inside her to live a new life. She has a map to make the drive down to the tip of South America, something she said she would do someday.

Roy wakes up dazed and confused from being drugged (it's a long story if you haven't seen the movie.) He looks around and tries to assess the situation.

> Roy: "What day is it?"
>
> June: "It's someday, Roy. It's someday."

Hey, it's time for *your* someday.

Go!

Epilogue:

Bumps in the Road Will Happen

You know it's a bad day when your fat pants are tight.

–Unknown

Having a bad day? Man, I had one today. I do a morning talk radio show every weekday from 5-9 a.m. I get to work at 3:30 a.m. and need every minute I have to read up on the latest news, research, outline the show, and get prepared.

I spend a couple of hours every night researching stories for the next day. I email them in a PDF document to myself so I can print them out at work. This morning, the file corrupted. It took me 15 minutes (instead of 30 seconds) to print it out.

My producer is on vacation, so I have different people filling in for him. Producing my show isn't just pushing a couple of buttons.

You have to know how to:

Cut and load sound bites in from newsmakers so I can play them on the show.

- Screen phone calls for the host.
- Manage the breaks with traffic, weather, advertisements, and news.
- Bump in and out of breaks on time—the timing must literally be down to the second.

The guy today didn't know how to do all that. Whoops. Not his fault. Just bad communication all around. So I had to train him on the fly. It made it hard for me to be truly prepared when the show started and throughout the show.

Several times during the morning I felt my blood pressure going up. I was starting to complain in my head and do the whole "why me?" bit.

But I've been working on having more joy in my life. I've read a few books on it and most agree that focusing on the things that are going well, and on the solutions to whatever problems you are facing, will help you feel a lot better than focusing on the problem. This doesn't mean you ignore the problem. Face the problem and find the solution.

I started listing in my head all the things that were going right.

When I came in this morning the printer had paper in it and it was working! (That's actually rarer than you would think.) My corrupted file did finally print. If it hadn't I would have lost two hours of work and not been as prepared for the show as I should be. The producer was working hard to get up to speed and to do what I needed. He had a good attitude. Everything was going to work out.

It worked. It helped me stay calm and enjoy my work. I had a good show and the listeners had no clue how hard the morning was.

No doubt I would have liked things to go differently this morning, but by focusing on solutions and what was going right, I was able to maintain my joy.

Good luck to you the next time your day isn't going so great. You can turn it around. It's a lot more fun than complaining, getting mad, and going around grumpy.

> *The only difference between a good day and a bad day is your attitude.*
>
> –Dennis S. Brown, author and speaker

Epilogue

If It Was Easy, Everyone Would Do It

I like work; it fascinates me. I can sit and look at it for hours.

–Jerome K. Jerome, writer and humorist

I know this seems like a lot of work. It is. It's a lot easier to coast through days, weeks, months, and years, never putting out the effort to live that extraordinary life. But that's not what you want or you would have stopped reading this a long time ago. You want something different. You are pursuing your Passionate Purpose. You are going to capitalize on that by increasing your income to the point you can change your family tree, give to others, live where you want, travel where and when you want, do what you want, and be financially free.

So when you get tired, or down, or you question yourself just remember, yes, all the hard work is worth it. If you do it right, you will also enjoy the entire journey.

I know it can be overwhelming to imagine that you are going to become the person who can do everything you must do to achieve all your dreams. It will take time. It will take effort. It won't go in a straight line. You will hit walls. But if you continually think about what you want and who you want to be, make a commitment to it, and consistently take action every day, you will succeed.

It's also OK if you don't want to do everything we've discussed here. Give yourself permission to pick and choose what works best for you. Don't reject everything we've talked about just because you don't like one or two ideas. That will leave you right where you were before you started reading my book. You weren't satisfied then, remember? Don't stick with the status quo. Get moving on *something* that will start you on the path pursuing your Passionate Purpose. After all, the years will go by either way. Do you want to look back twenty years from now and say I just kept making a living, or do you want to look back and say that was when I decided to start making an *extraordinary* life?

Go!

My hope for you is that you get started right now on your Passionate Purpose. What are you waiting for?

Go. Now.

Why are you still sitting there? Go!

My Story

I've given you glimpses into my life throughout this book. Here is the story of how I got into radio and went from having no education, training, or experience in the field to hosting a nationally syndicated talk show in just nine years.

Burned Out

I was getting burned out in the mental health field and realized I needed to do something else. I wasn't pursuing happiness. With a master's degree in counseling psychology I didn't think I was qualified to do much outside of the field. I decided I'd go into sales. I left the house one morning, telling my wife I would be a cellular telephone salesman by the end of the day. This was in 1996 and cell phones were really on the way up.

But something stopped me from taking that job. It was the idea inside me that I needed to pursue my Passionate Purpose.

Don't get me wrong. I understand that sometimes you have to take a job you don't like. I took a job digging ditches just to keep money coming in while I was waiting for my background check to clear for my mental health counseling job. I had a master's degree and I was earning five dollars an hour digging ditches. I did what millions of Americans do every day—work at a job they hate to pay the bills.

But I knew in my heart that I could create a career doing what I loved. I knew if I did that I would make more than enough to provide for my family while I was also pursuing happiness.

> *Do what you love. When you love your work, you become the best worker in the world.*
>
> –Uri Geller, illusionist, author

I Get Paid to Talk on the Radio

Nothing happens unless first we dream.

–Carl Sandburg, poet, writer

I had no idea how to break in to the radio business. So I called up the number one news talk station in Jacksonville, FL, WOKV. I told the operations manager that I wanted to work in talk radio, and I would do anything they needed done to get my foot in the door. I had no idea what to expect. I had no training in radio. I had no education in radio. I had no idea how I could help this radio station at all. But I had a dream and the passion to pursue it.

When I made my pitch to the operations manager there was silence on the other end of the phone for about a second. Then this: "Can you be here by five o'clock today?" That was it. I had my entry-level job in talk radio making minimum wage. I kept my day job in the mental health world and added a nighttime shift in radio. I started off producing recorded shows. And by "producing," I mean making sure all of the commercials ran on time. After proving myself for a couple months, I was made a producer of a live call-in show on the company's new sports talk channel.

I was learning a lot about how radio works, but I wasn't even close to getting on the air. I told the program director what my dreams were in radio. He wasn't impressed with my plans and told me to keep producing. I did, but I also started practicing my talk radio show. At the end of my shift when almost no one was in the building, I would sneak into one of the studios and record myself doing a mock talk radio show. I would listen to the tapes of myself on the way home from work. I knew enough about talk radio to know what was good and what wasn't. And at first I was horrible. But I kept at it and after a few weeks I thought my show started to sound OK.

I was getting paid around seven dollars an hour to do my radio-producing gig, and of course I wasn't getting paid at all to do my pretend show. But sometimes you have to work for free or for very little money in order to reach your goal.

Everyone talks about how much money Tiger Woods makes in one day when he wins a golf tournament. But he isn't making that money in one day. He is getting paid back for every hour and every day he spent on the golf course from the age of three developing his skills. He practiced and played the game of golf for 17 years before he started getting paid to play. That's what I was doing in radio. I was paying my dues.

I was starting to make friends in the radio business, and some of them were kind enough to critique my tapes. With their input, and more practice, I started to develop my own style. I thought I was ready. I took my best tape to the program director and asked him if I could go on the air. I'm not really sure if he actually listened to the tape, but he told me to get back to producing. It was pretty clear that my program director had no intention of ever letting me get on the air. I was a producer, period.

That wasn't my dream. My dream was to be the host of my own talk show. My dream was to give everyone my opinion and to have people call in and challenge me on the air. My dream was to become a nationally syndicated talk show host. My dream was to write opinion columns for newspapers and magazines. My dream was to become a paid speaker. After about a year of producing, I knew I was going to have to do something drastic to pursue those dreams.

There was a very small station in Jacksonville, WZNZ. It simulcasted the CNN Headline News television feed on the radio all day long. The station had zero ratings. It was not making money. I made an appointment with the general sales manager and explained to him that I wanted to do a talk show during afternoon drive time. He told me I could do it if I would buy the airtime. I was so new in talk radio I didn't even understand that this happened all the time.

The good news was this was a way I could get on the air. The bad news was I had to pay $200 an hour to be on a station that no one was listening to. The other bad news was I would have to quit one of my jobs in order to spend the time required to prepare and do a good talk show and sell advertising to pay for the show. Even more bad news was that my wife, Anne, and I weren't rolling in the dough. We were going to have to use our savings to pay for my airtime. I was really worried about that. I was pretty confident I could sell enough advertising to pay for my time on the station, but if I couldn't, I would feel like I was letting my wife down. My wife didn't even hesitate. She told me to go for it. She's the best.

I wanted to do a three-hour show every weekday. That would mean I would owe the station $3,000 a week. No way. I settled for a one-hour show every weekday. It turned out to be a very wise decision. Because WZNZ did not have an audience, it was very difficult to sell advertising on the station. I visited every mom-and-pop store in Jacksonville. Most of the storeowners didn't even want to talk to me. The ones who did couldn't see the value in buying airtime on my show. They were right. There was no value in buying airtime on my show … yet.

For the first few weeks of my show I didn't receive a single telephone call. I didn't have any guests. It was just my opinions and me for an hour every weekday. I started having friends call in the show so it wasn't just my voice for the whole hour. I didn't tell them what to say. They were real calls with their real opinions, but it wasn't the same as having new listeners call in.

It wasn't going well. I had gone from doing a show for free to paying someone to let me do a show. When was I actually going to start making money?

Because I was still new at all this, I had a ton to learn. I was spending about four hours every weekday getting ready for a one-hour radio show. I had to know what I was talking about and there was a lot of news to read every day. I was also reading books on history, current events, politics, and how to do good radio. I was spending several more hours every day trying to sell advertising time on the show. No one was listening and no one was buying airtime. I was eating up the savings my wife and I had worked so hard to earn. I felt like I was letting Anne down. Part of me wanted to give up.

But another part of me was strangely excited. Even with all the bad things happening I was really enjoying my time on the radio. I was coming up with interesting angles on the big news stories, making up comedy bits, and writing parody songs. I was learning how to do good talk radio without depending on callers. I was studying how to be a good salesperson. And then something funny happened. People started calling the show. New listeners, not just my friends, were calling the show.

After four months on the air at WZNZ, my show was the highest ranked hour of the day for the station. I had an audience. The bad news was I was also quickly running out of money. I told the general sales manager that I could not continue paying for the show. He told me he was impressed with my rating success, and he didn't want to lose me. From that point on, I no longer had to pay for my airtime. I was now on the air from 4 to 6 p.m. every weekday. I still wasn't getting paid, but I no longer had to pay to get on the air.

My workday now consisted of four hours of show prep and research, two hours on the air, and four to five hours trying to sell advertising time for the show. To supplement our income I was working nights at the mental health clinic doing intake assessments on involuntary patients. I was also constantly trying to become a better talk show host.

After nine months of this, I still wasn't making any money on the radio. My wife was bringing in everything we needed to live on, I was bringing in my part-time salary, but I felt like I wasn't pulling my weight. I told Anne that if something didn't happen soon I was going to have to quit radio and get a real job.

Then a little God wink happened. I received a call from the program director at WOKV. My old boss had noticed my rating success at WZNZ and was offering me a job to host a local talk show weeknights from 7 to 10 p.m.

I saw this as my big break. I was going to be on the number one talk show station in Jacksonville. I would have tens of thousands of people listening to me. And I would get paid to do it. It turned out I would get paid a whopping $18,000 a year, but at least I was getting paid.

I started thinking about how amazing my life was. It was amazing that I lived in a country that allowed me to pursue my Passionate Purpose. It was amazing that God had led me to my beautiful wife, Anne. It was amazing how often I seemed to be in the right place at the right time for my radio career. It was amazing how all my hard work was paying off. I had a lot to be grateful for.

My show on WOKV grew quickly. I had more than enough calls coming in to keep the show sounding fresh. My ratings were good and continued to get better. The station hired a consultant who told the program director I should be on in the afternoon drive spot from 3-6 p.m. My show was soon ranked number one in the demographic for men 35 to 64 years old. But I was still very naïve about the radio business. I was only making $20,000 a year, and I wasn't even working under a contract.

A Child and Some Moves

About a year later I was offered the morning show at a station in Gainesville, Florida. I didn't really want to move. The salary would be slightly higher, but the main reason I took the job was that WOKV had brought in some syndicated programming and pushed my show back an hour. I figured that if they were going to bump my show when I was number one in the market, what would they do if my ratings slipped to number two?

By this time my wife and I had our first child, Faith. Anne was teaching at an elementary school and did not want to move until the school year was out. We decided I would commute to Gainesville until then. My show would start at 6 a.m., so driving an hour and a half to Gainesville every morning didn't make much sense. Instead, I asked the general manager of WSKY in Gainesville if I could sleep on the conference room floor for the next two months until my family moved with me to Gainesville. He laughed and said sure. I guess he thought I was kidding. I wasn't.

For the next two months I'd roll out my sleeping bag in the conference room of the station to get some sleep. I would be up at 3 a.m. to research and prepare the show. I would do my show from 6-9 a.m., take care of any meetings with clients, and then immediately drive to Jacksonville and pick up Faith from her babysitter.

Anne would get home around four o'clock in the afternoon. We would spend time together, eat dinner, put Faith to bed, and around nine o'clock at night I would drive back to Gainesville to sleep on the conference room floor. At 3 a.m. I would wake up and do it all over again.

After about a month of this the general manager called me into his office. He said he heard a rumor that I was sleeping at the office. I told him it was true and that he had personally given me permission to do it. His response was, “You were serious about that?” He made me promise not to tell anyone else about it over his concerns that the station might get in trouble for allowing me to use it as my flop house.

I still didn’t have a contract because I didn’t even know that most talk show hosts worked with contracts. I later learned that the best ones were multi-year contracts. This gave the host security. He knew that if he did his job and kept his nose clean, he would be paid for the duration of his contract even if his ratings went down and/or the station fired him. Instead, I was working without a contract, which meant the station could fire me at any time for any reason. I think someone up there was looking out for me because my lack of a contract would actually help me in the very near future.

I was still learning a lot about how to be a good talk show host and my show was still improving. The next ratings book showed that I was number one in the station’s target demographic. I was really happy with how the show was sounding, I had a great relationship with my program director, Andrew Lee, but I still wanted to be a nationally syndicated host.

I didn’t understand yet how difficult it was to become nationally syndicated so I just started calling syndicators to ask them if they wanted to hire me. When I told them I was currently a morning talk show host in Gainesville, Florida, a few of them laughed out loud at me. Thankfully, I didn’t let that bother me. I did get the message, however. I would need to get on the air in a bigger market before any syndicator would seriously look at my show.

Around that time I received a call that would be my next big break. It would introduce me to the best program director I have ever worked for. He taught me more about talk radio than anyone else and he became a good friend. Jeff Hillery from KLIF in Dallas had heard about me from a friend of his in Jacksonville. Jeff was trying to rebuild the station. It had been through a lot of turnover during the past few years and the ratings had dropped precipitously. That didn’t bother me at all. I had no doubt I could increase the ratings. I expected to be number one in the market in a couple years. I wasn't really cocky, just confident. I had no idea how different market #5 Dallas was from market #81 Gainesville or even market #46 Jacksonville.

I didn't really want to move to Dallas. Both my wife's family and my family were in Florida. We had a two and a half-year-old daughter and another one on the way. I wanted my children to know their cousins and their grandparents. My wife asked me why we should move and I told her we had 80,000 reasons. That was the pay that was offered to me by KLIF. It seemed like $1 million to me at the time. It was almost four times what I was currently making. Plus, I wouldn't have to wake up at three o'clock in the morning anymore. In reality, that was a very low salary for an afternoon talk show host in the fifth biggest market in America. But I didn't know any better. With that salary my wife could quit her job teaching and stay home with our children until they were school-aged, and I would be one step closer to my dream of national syndication.

I was on an adrenaline high. In four years I had gone from having zero experience in the radio business to landing a prime-time spot on the air in Dallas.

This time I signed a contract. I had a two-year deal with KLIF. Jeff took me under his wing and really showed me how to be a professional talk show host. I had the personality, information, and entertainment part of the show down. But I had never really been taught all the details about radio formatics. They are the little things that listeners don't notice when you do them but often quit listening to you when you don't do them.

We had a lot of talent on that station. Darryl Ankarlo was our morning host and he excelled at taking a local issue and making it his.

Our noon–3 p.m. man was Scott Anderson. He was just a super nice guy, and that came through your radio.

I had the afternoon drive slot. I was having the time of my life on the radio. I was getting paid well to do things I loved to do. I would get up in the morning and spend a couple hours reading stories on the Internet. Then I would eat breakfast with my wife and kids, go work out, spend another couple hours prepping for the show at work, and then give my opinions on the biggest stories of the day. Listeners would call in and debate me. I was interviewing senators, former presidents, and regular people who were part of the stories I was discussing on the show.

I was talking to more people than I ever had in my life. As our ratings grew, I realized that during any 15 minutes of my program I was talking to the number of people who would fill up Texas Stadium. I thought that was pretty cool.

The people in the Metroplex of Dallas/Fort Worth were just like the people in the South I'd grown up with. They were friendly and always looking to help you. My wife started making friends very quickly. The only things we missed about living in north Texas were our family and the beach.

I was with KLIF for five years, building the ratings. When I first arrived the station had a .9 share with people 12 and older. We more than doubled those ratings. That might not sound like a big jump, but it was. The increase in our ratings in our target demographic was even greater. The station had gone from losing money to making a healthy profit.

I was getting some of my opinion articles published in *The Dallas Morning News* and on political websites. Fox News Channel and CNN had me on as a guest. Things were really rolling along.

Around that time a new company bought KLIF and our cluster of stations. A lot of good people were let go. My program director saw what was coming and took a great job at Fox News Radio. It looked to me like the station was moving in the wrong direction. It was time to pursue other opportunities. I had some interest from some other stations and some good markets. But I really wanted to pursue my dream of national syndication, and get back to Florida.

During my years in Dallas I had started making contact with the national syndicators again. I would periodically send them some of my demo tapes. I was able to fill in for nationally syndicated hosts Glenn Beck, Tony Snow, and G. Gordon Liddy. That experience made me confident I was ready to be nationally syndicated.

After a lot of work I signed a contract for a nationally syndicated weekday show from 3 to 6 p.m. Eastern Time. I was stoked.

My family was a little sad to leave Dallas. We loved the people and we loved the town. But we were very excited to get back to Florida, our families, and the beach. I hadn't used my surfboard in five years!

We moved back to Jacksonville, and found a home just four miles from the ocean. I set up a studio in the den and did the show from there every weekday. My commute to the office was a five-second walk from the bedroom to my studio.

I almost couldn't believe it. Could it really have been only nine years ago that I called up WOKV and asked if I could do anything to get into the radio business?

> *All who have accomplished great things have had a great aim, have fixed their gaze on a goal which was high, one which sometimes seemed impossible.*
>
> –Orison Swett Marden, author

I was blessed. But none of that would have happened if I had not decided to pursue happiness. Looking back on that journey I'm even more amazed that I succeeded. I did have a goal, but I never really sat down and outlined how I was going to achieve that goal. I pretty much just made it up as I went along. But the fact that I had a goal and I was pursuing my passion with all my might to achieve it helped work everything else out.

I started to wonder what would happen if I became even more specific on my goals. What if I expanded my pursuit of happiness to every aspect of my life? What if I started to pursue my Passionate Purpose? What can happen if you do?

I've been applying many of the principles in this book for years in my own life. They have helped me get where I wanted to go faster than I ever thought possible. I had a very limiting mindset about my vocation and income when I was in high school, college, and when I entered the work force. Reading and practicing the techniques of the masters has changed my mindset and changed my life.

My Story

Every time I reach a goal, my mind is expanded to even bigger goals. Better yet, as long as I'm pursuing my Passionate Purpose, I'm enjoying the process of learning, becoming a better person, and accomplishing things I wouldn't have dreamed of just a few years ago.

I still don't reach my goals in a straight line. There are days I forget to practice what I preach. I forget to plan. I forget to set daily goals to reach my yearly goals and I become overwhelmed. Then, my accountability friend reminds me to refocus on my why and all the great techniques in this book I've been using for years. They work! As long as you keep moving forward, you will succeed.

Why not you? You can do it.

Go!

About the Author

Here's what I think you might want to know about me if you're about to read, or you've already read my book.

If you're trying to find your Passionate Purpose I am your soul brother. All my life I've been seeking that and trying to live it out. When I was still in high school I told my friends I didn't want to live a mediocre life. The idea of just being average and going through the motions until I finally died petrified me.

The good news is I have found more than one purpose in my life and I keep finding new ones. I'm pursuing my Passionate Purpose more than I ever have and I keep getting happier while doing it.

My next book will include how fun it is to keep living out the things on my bucket list. I hope to include some of your stories as well.

I am a Christian, husband, father, son, friend, radio host, speaker, coach, trainer, blogger, author, surfer, guitar player, and lover of martial arts films (subtitled, not dubbed).

I am married to an incredibly supportive wife who puts up with all my dreams and ideas. I have two talented daughters who remind me to slow down and enjoy right where I am, right now.

I would love to hear how this book helps you on your journey and answer your questions. My email is gregorybknapp@gmail.com

My blog is http://gregorybknapp.com/

Follow me on Twitter: https://twitter.com/gregorybknapp

Thanks for giving me your most precious asset, your time. Enjoy the pursuit.

Greg Knapp

Notes

Chapter 5. You Are Talented and Lucky Enough

[1] Geoff Colvin, *Talent Is Overrated: What Really Separates World-Class Performers from Everybody Else* (London: Nicholas Brealey Publishing, 2009), 66

[2] Daniel Coyle, *The Talent Code: Greatness Isn't Born. It's Grown. Here's How* (New York: Random House, 2009), 92

Chapter 6. Mindset

[1] Carol Dweck, *Mindset: The New Psychology of Success* (New York: Random House, 2006), 13

Go!

Made in the USA
Charleston, SC
23 December 2016